THE BROKEN APPLE

THE BROKEN APPLE

New York City in the 1980s

Herbert London

Transaction Publishers

New Brunswick (U.S.A.) and London (U.K.)

Library of Congress Catalog Number: 89-4446
ISBN: 0-88738-296-7
Printed in the United States of America

Library of Congress Cataloging-in-Publication Data
London, Herbert Ira.
    The broken apple: New York City in the 1980s / Herbert London
    p. cm.
    ISBN 0-88738-296-7
    1. New York (N.Y.)—Social conditions. 2. New York (N.Y.)—Economic
conditions. I. Title.
HN80.N5L66 1989
306'.09747'109048—dc20   89-4446
                                                                   CIP

To the women in my life—my wife, my daughters, my mom, my aunt

Contents

Introduction

If Paris was *the* city of the eighteenth century and London was *the* city of the nineteenth century, New York is unquestionably *the* city of the twentieth century. It is a city of almost unimaginable opulence, a place electric with possibility, the setting for technological wonders that scrape the heavens, and the acknowledged center for opportunity. Yet amid the wealth and the technological marvels is another city, a city that resembles Dante's *Inferno*. This is the place of the underclass, an ambience of dope and violence, horrors that defy the imagination, and a fascination with consumption. It is unsettling to think that, as with Tom Wolfe's character Sherman McCoy, one wrong turn on the highway can alter one's comfortable existence into the dark and unpredictable world of incivility and barbarism.

As many social critics have noted, the New York of the 1940s and 1950s is light years away from the city of today. If the earlier New York was at the apogee of its evolution, New York today is in the *fin de siècle*. It is still a city of enormous promise and prosperity, but it is also a town battered by crime, negative publicity, high prices, and standstill traffic. Perhaps more than any other city in the Western world, New York is an anachronism. It continues to maintain confidence in the ability of government to provide services and manage significant aspects of the local economy. While other nations and municipalities have come to appreciate the effects of privatization, New York is rooted in New Deal philosophy, a system predicated on the belief that that government is best which rules most.

In this town of 7 million stories almost anything one says is true. The art is more experimental, the mood swings more erratic, the class stratification more extreme, the quotidian existence more brutal than in other places. Yet most New Yorkers won't give it up even when offered an alternative. New Yorkers are a tough breed. They are easily identified in other places because the city is in their blood. They are fast on their feet and with their mouths. They are impertinent. They are warm and they are forthright. They speak with New York accents as a sign of honor. And they are blessed with eternal hope.

There is in this distinctly New York ointment a fly larger than might ordinarily be expected. While New Yorkers are more adaptable than almost any people on earth, there is only so much chaos the human spirit can endure. The social, cultural, economic, educational, criminal, and political conditions have conspired to make much of this city a Dickensian nightmare of random violence, ubiquitous filth, and congestion. New York may indeed be an unintended laboratory for pushing human stress to its limit.

As a born-and-bred New Yorker who has benefited from and occasionally been frustrated by life in this town, I have been recording my observations for about ten years in such local publications as the *New York Post*, *New York Times*, *New York Daily News*, *Newsday*, *Staten Island Eagle*, and *New York City Tribune*. In most respects these articles, written primarily in the 1980s, reflect what was uppermost in my mind at the time they were written. Each is a snapshot of the city; in the aggregate these articles are a montage of the decade, what may well be called the Koch years by some urban historian in the future.

The articles are organized by category in order to give coherence to this seemingly random exercise. In fact, the categories are arbitrary and there is unquestionably some overlap. Nonetheless, the pieces were carefully selected and represent fewer than a fifth of those written during this period. In my opinion they represent a mood that is one part personal, one part journalistic, and one part distinctly New Yorkish.

As I reread these articles it occurred to me that my fascination with New York and my own political aspiration emerged from doing the research, thinking, and writing that went into these articles. The idea of a kid from Coney Island serving as dean at New York University and then running for mayor, as a Republican no less, demonstrates a great deal about the spirit of this city. That spirit is an intrinsic part of this collection.

Over these years I've had the good fortune to work with several excellent editors. None, however, measure up to Irving Louis Horowitz, the distinguished sociologist, and Mary Curtis. I am equally indebted to my friend Peter Shaw who is invariably an inspiration for ideas and a continual source of brilliant insights about the city. I am also deeply grateful to my wife who patiently understands my compulsive need to put on paper what I rarely utter at the dinner table and to my children, Staci, Nancy, and Jaclyn, who let me write even when they wanted my advice on a term paper or a bedtime story.

In the final analysis I shall hide behind the bromide that the ideas in this book are mine. I shall certainly take the heat. But it might also be noted that the ideas in this collection emerge from New York, from my perception of New York. My notions of this town are found on the streets, in the theaters, below ground in the subway, above ground in the skyscrapers, in the noise, in the grime, and in the sweet rhapsodies that accompany the convergence of night and day in the city that never sleeps.

Part I

Cultural Life in the City

1

New Yorkers Reach for the Sky in Their Ever Restless Quest

The bidding that is now taking place for a contract to construct a tower on the site of the New York Coliseum raises some interesting questions about this city and perhaps about our national vision. There are many things one can say about New York including and especially the fact that uncivil behavior is ubiquitous. But it is also true that New York captures the tempo of the nation. It throbs with energy; it is electric.

It is not coincidental that several of the real estate barons developed plans for a tower taller than the Sears building in Chicago, the world's tallest. New Yorkers don't want to be outdone. The city's vision is toward the heavens, to the ephemeral. Perhaps for that reason it is a place with a truncated memory. Our memorials are razed; the places of our youth disappear or are transmogrified into new forms. The Polo Grounds and Ebbets Field are housing projects. That is a stain on my memory of Willie Mays and Jackie Robinson. There is no tyranny of the grave here. New Yorkers quickly forget their past.

The French writer Jacques Maritain made the observation that on every trip to New York he found a new city. The store he was fond of frequenting was gone, replaced by another. A seemingly sturdy building was torn down to make room for an even more sturdy edifice. The impression was created that each year New Yorkers tear down their city to build a new one. Infrequent visitors to New York invariably have this impression. Certainly it is not disabused when the old Metropolitan Opera House is torn down or the Coliseum faces extinction.

This lack of confidence in tradition can be an asset. We are not transfixed by the way conditions were. Change is our ally; when market factors are transformed, our city follows suit. New York is an ode to capitalism. Daniel Boorstin, the historian, made the observation that this nation is in a state of "becoming." That description aptly captures the spirit of this city.

3

How quickly that temple of ingenuity on 34th Street called the Empire State Building has been replaced in our encomiums by the World Trade Center, the Sears building, and an as-yet-unnamed building that will rise above them all. The competition to rise to a new height, to be the one who builds the tallest building, is a city obsession. In Paris no one would care about such *jejune* pursuits. It is quickly labeled an expression of American Pollyannas. Yet Parisians in New York cannot take their eyes off our skyline. It is hypnotic, especially for those who want to explore the future.

Zbigniev Brezinski, the erstwhile national security adviser, made the point that the United States has been to the future. For every explorer who searches for the answer to tomorrow, New York is the laboratory. There is no other place with the intensity of experience found here. To be a New Yorker is the opposite of "laid back." New Yorkers don't need caffeine to wake up—the city is their alarm.

Somewhere in the thickets of midtown offices, an architect is playfully sketching a dream tower that will ultimately jut into the heavens. New Yorkers expect that in five years, perhaps ten, a new shiny edifice will present itself to our skyline. The Empire State Building, by the way, was built in one year; obviously construction is slower in the future. But a faith that this new structure will appear is inextinguishable. In New York, one expects the unexpected, the biggest, the most lavish, the glitziest, the most outlandish, the future. This future isn't always salutary. It takes its toll in early deaths and overactivity. But it is also true that, as Samuel Johnson said of nineteenth-century London, there is in New York "all that life can afford."

That tower over the corpse of the Coliseum bespeaks our dreams yet to come. It reminds us that New York can be cruel and bitter, but it is always imaginative, always looking skyward.

July 13, 1985

2

Changing Our Street Names

Consistent with the 100th anniversary of the birth of Jamaican national hero Marcus Garvey, Mayor Edward Koch signed a bill into law that changes the name of Sumner Avenue in Brooklyn to Marcus Garvey Avenue. In principle there is certainly nothing wrong with such a name change. After all, if Horace Harding Boulevard can become the Long Island Expressway, one should not expect place names to exist in perpetuity. Moreover, there is often good reason to change a street name. Garvey preached black pride and respect for Africa, which in themselves are sufficient for recognition. The unseemly aspects of his life and proclamations can, at least for the moment, be ignored.

What gives me pause is not the change of name or the selection of Garvey as the honoree; rather, it is the unintentional rewriting or dismissal of history. Sumner Avenue was originally called Yates Avenue. It was renamed in 1881 to honor a New England abolitionist, Massachusetts Senator Charles Sumner who was among the most vocal critics of slavery.

It seems to me that Sumner should have a street named after him. If Garvey is honored, so too should Charles Sumner. The problem, of course, is that both men cannot be honored on the same avenue. But this problem is easy to resolve if every Elm, Maple, Oak Street or First, Second, Third Avenue or Main Street were the thoroughfares selected for name change. Why inter Sumner Avenue when there are so many appropriate candidates available for a change in name? Admittedly, Sumner doesn't have a vocal constituency that wants to see his name survive. But if Garvey replaces him, it is unlikely any youngster will ask, "Who was that Sumner anyway?"

I have no particular animus to trees; and numbered avenues do add clarity to addresses. But I much prefer names attached to streets than descriptions. Let us use our streets to honor heroes, those that future generations should remember, recognizing full well that this can be a tricky business. Houston (pronounced Howston) Street in lower Manhattan doesn't honor Sam Houston. If you should be a Texan visiting New York, you wouldn't know

5

that. Should you ask for Houston Street, a taxi driver will take you to Euston Street, pronounced as if it were named after the hero of the Alamo. This can, and often does, cause consternation among visitors. But it is a small price to pay for the sustenance of our national heroes.

If we get in the business of substituting one figure for another, as was the case with Garvey and Sumner, the historical price one pays is not trivial. In this case value judgments and political considerations are critical and very often enter the realm of a Hobson's choice. Should Truman be displaced by Kennedy? And if so, on what grounds? If a black hero replaces a white hero, is this done to mollify the residents of the community at the moment? Indeed, if this practice is valid, should the street name be changed again when the population becomes Chinese or Hispanic?

Under these circumstances the city would require a commission authorized to review street names on the basis of ethnic distribution. Brighton Beach Avenue, for example, should have been recast in the last years as Solzhenitsyn Avenue. Delancey Street should be called Sun Yat-sen Street. Needless to say, this might make living in New York even more complicated than it is at the moment.

If the purpose of changing street names is to give young people a sense of their history, then continual change only encourages historicism—the belief that what comes after is necessarily better than what came before. Surely, encouraging remembrance is a desirable act, particularly for those men and women whose deeds should be seared into our collective memory. It makes no sense to act like our Soviet counterparts creating nonpersons for each new generation. Erasing names from street signs has its inexact analogue in eliminating names from history texts.

I'm not sure where Charles Sumner Avenue should be located. Yet I am sure there should be a Sumner Avenue. Since New Yorkers don't easily change their habits, it is conceivable that many residents of Brooklyn will continue to call Garvey Avenue, Sumner Avenue. I don't know of one New Yorker who calls Sixth Avenue, Avenue of the Americas. So Sumner may have a life after erasure. But this is certainly no way to treat our heroes or to encourage a respect for history.

October 29, 1987

3

Ten Miles of Great Rides
Right in Manhattan

With Coney Island having decayed beyond repair, New York lacks a good, old-fashioned amusement park. Perhaps that explains why the East Side River Drive, sometimes known as the FDR Drive, has been converted into one—ten miles of exciting rides.

At 96th Street, one gets on the loop-de-loop, a ride that takes you up to a precipice as you bound up and down in your car. From 96th Street to 86th Street, it's the House of Horrors, a dark region with narrow lanes where steering is precarious. Near 61st Street, the rides comes to a halt any time of night or day. Enjoy the crawl through man-made craters near 59th Street.

At the United Nations, one again enters the Dark Region, a netherland that never is lit. This is followed by the "serpentine mile" of sharp and blind curves. Just when one assumes clear sailing ahead, there is the bumper car ride near New York University Hospital, where cars enter the highway and try to bang into your vehicle. At 21st Street, the bumps in the road turn into ridges. Tires grind and shriek. Below Houston Street, the obstacle course begins. What I used to think was temporary construction is in fact a permanent feature of the park.

During the winter, waves from the East River wash over the road barriers and spray your car as you travel uptown. And when spring showers arrive, water will rise above tire level in the dark, low-lying regions going downtown. Even the routes off the highway provide surprises. There is the Turtle Crawl at the 96th Street exit. Some people who exited last April are still there. The 71st Street exit is a surprise, since it appears to be a continuation of the highway. However, if you remain in the right lane, you soon find yourself exiting.

To ensure safety, the park has holes everywhere, so that any driver traveling more than thirty miles per hour will assuredly break an axle. Rarely does anyone get hurt. Should even a minor accident occur, the safety of all riders is assured. No one really moves.

The most important feature of this ride is that it is free. You don't even have to have a ticket. What I don't understand is why Mayor Edward Koch doesn't advertise this amusement park the way Orlando, Florida, publicized Disney World. We have everything Orlando has and more. The thrills are at least the equal of Space Mountain. Most people who leave FDR Amusement Park mumble, ''That was some ride.'' It's unfortunate that New Yorkers who have so many competing attractions, don't appreciate this one. Maybe one day when it looks as dilapidated as the West Side Highway, we'll come to understand its value.

November 8, 1986

4

Let's End Public Funding
of Demoralizing Art

The call is out. Artists are now mobilizing once again to apply pressure on the government to provide additional subsidies to the arts. Alvin Lane, a lawyer specializing in the legal aspects of art, wrote in the *New York Times* on July 13, 1985: "If we leave the selection of public art to residents of a community—or even permit their strong influence in the process—we will end up with an esthetic common denominator of sterile, benign and conventionalized art that will neither offend nor stimulate anyone." Presumably, the purpose of this government-sponsored art will cultivate the public's appreciation of "fine" art. But where is the evidence for this claim.

Richard Serra's 112-foot metal sculpture "Tilted Arc" was generally scorned by the public when it was placed in New York's Federal Plaza. Its removal has sparked a public debate about the subsidized muse, but it has not changed skepticism about modern art.

And who can blame the average person? Public art may be innovative but in most cases it represents an artistic sensibility the average person doesn't share. Elitists and those aficionados of modern art will argue that the public must be educated. However, it is very difficult to contend—although some critics do—that the conventional taste of average people is any less desirable than the guidelines established by the General Services Administration or even a panel of "recognized" art experts. Art, by its very nature is personal. The humor and modern language some see in an Oldenberg sculpture are perceived as trash by others. Who is right?

The key question is why should a group of experts use tax-levied funds to impose an artistic sensibility on a reluctant public. Certainly one can't be sure the imposition of taste is good for it. Nor can one argue that there is a universal standard by which artistic judgment is made. One is entrapped by subjectivity. That isn't a problem when personal choice is permitted. But in

9

the case of public art, tax dollars are employed to impose a vision of art that the experts believe is one we need.

Lane writes: "A panel's findings should not be based solely on the artist's esthetic achievement but should also take account of the needs and desires of the community itself." By whose authority does this panel speak for a community in which it wants to place modern artifacts?

Since the establishment of arts councils at the federal and state levels, I can find virtually no convincing evidence that in the aggregate the artistic life of this nation is more vigorous than it was before the creation of these government dispensers of public funds. Moreover, if anything, my sensibilities suggest that the arts have tilted in the other direction. Almost every major city has some monolithic monstrosity in front of a public building. My guess is that if the choice of public monuments were put to a vote the average person would prefer a replica of Michelangelo's "David." Admittedly the choice would be conventional. But I find it difficult to accept the argument that this replica isn't more aesthetically desirable than an original sculpture of a lipstick tube. The average person is right to resist the snobbish standard of the art expert who equates the avant garde with what the public should appreciate.

Another problem with public art is that it can't be hidden. In order to have it removed a public outcry has to reach the halls of Congress. An ugly artifact stands as an affront to public taste. It is a reminder that some group believes it knows what is good for you. It's presence in a public square also suggests an artistic standard by which the young make future judgments of the arts. What can a steel monolith possibly suggest about the spirit of humankind?

If we are going to use tax dollars to promote public art—then I think the public, not some panel of artists, should be making the decisions. But that is my back-up position. It seems to me that the art people acquire is related to personal taste. Let people buy what they want. Let the government stay out of the art business. Let my tax dollars be used to defend our liberty and not offend public sensibilities. If in the process some talented artists, whose work does not receive public acclamation, are left behind, so be it. That is still a small price to pay compared to the undemocratic club art experts wield and the spread of unconventional artistic ugliness that now afflicts our cities.

August 15, 1985

5

Don't Ruin Our Beautiful Buildings

Several years ago a young woman passing an old building in New York was struck and killed by masonry that fell from that edifice. That incident and several similar ones are responsible for changing the face of New York. An ordinance was passed requiring the repair or removal of defective building outcroppings.

In part, this legislation was a response to possible injury. It was also a reaction to financial liability should someone get hurt from falling masonry. As a consequence, some of the loveliest buildings in New York are enshrouded in dismal scaffolding, often latticed with barbed wire to discourage burglars. Landmarks such as the Mayflower Hotel on Central Park West have become aesthetic prisoners to the local ordinance. And it looks to me as if "removal" rather than "repair" is the common response to the ordinance.

Denuding older buildings of true architectural grandeur diminishes the city. What remains untouched are the modern Bauhaus boxes that carefully avoid carved façades. Intricate detail, gargoyles—all of the artistic "extras" worthy of notice. It is instructive that when Woody Allen wanted to give his audience a sense of Manhattan life in *Hannah and Her Sisters*, he put together a montage of photographs from the façades of older buildings, pre-World War II structures.

The vitality of this city is difficult to measure. But one aspect of it is the building façades that keep visitors transfixed. A Chrysler Building is forever a source of wonderment—its gargoyles jutting out as if to warn trespassers about the dangers on the street below. The Woolworth Building, while dwarfed by the new structures in the financial district, has much more character than its would-be competitors for architectural greatness. By comparison, the World Trade Center is a hollow shell that couldn't even attract the attention of a King Kong.

My concern about the aesthetic quality of city life does not mean that I am unaware of the danger associated with loose masonry. What I'm suggesting,

11

however, is that our legislators overreacted to the problem and have unwittingly affected the central aesthetic of New York life adversely.

Life in this city can be difficult even when there are magnificent buildings to capture our attention. But when we reduce building façades to barren slabs of concrete or remove the curlicues and fascinating detail that give buildings distinction, we are in fact suggesting that people can be reduced to the lowest common living space, that our surroundings are inconsequential.

In a city that puts a premium on individuality, our unique buildings and façades constitute a measure of urban vitality. It is a shame that much of what we value aesthetically in this city is being diminished.

August 28,1986

6

The New Central Park Zoo:
A Tribute to the Absurd

Going to the zoo is a rite of passage for the young. What this experience offers children is the live version of animals in their books. *Where the Wild Things Are* is transmogrified from fiction to reality. It is also the case that the animals in a zoo offer a stark contrast with civilized society. Youngsters can stare at a lion and know intuitively that they are confronting a fierce, primordial nature, a gulf of unbridgeable proportions. A child doesn't require a description of the animal kingdom—as so often occurs in the modern zoo— to know what distinguishes animals from humankind.

Yet the renovated zoo at Central Park defies this distinction. What has been built is a habitat that disguises the difference between human and animal. Instead of a nature presented in primordial form is the sanitized version of an ecosystem in which human and animal systems are inextricably linked. The architects at the new Central Park Zoo have made a concerted effort to suggest that flora and fauna are uniform, the web that ties life together on this globe.

Hidden from view is the political judgment on which the new zoo is constructed. The Central Park Zoo is a paean to the religion of environmentalism, which casts humans as one of God's many creatures. Characteristics of humans that differentiate us from the animal kingdom are intentionally glossed over or ignored. On the other hand, the animals are made anthropomorphic. Only those that resemble humans in their relative gentleness appear in the new zoo. The lions, elephants, tigers, panthers, and hippos are gone. What remains are seals, rabbits, and monkeys.

Zoo keepers in the new age argue that it was "inhumane" to keep the king of the jungle caged in a cubicle. Yet whenever lions nurtured in a zoo are allowed to roam free they return to self-constructed cages. Apparently it is not the lion who finds confinement inhumane. This is yet another of those environmental myths fed an unwary people. It is obviously easier for beasts to be given food each day by zoo attendants than to have to find prey in the wild African plains.

From my point of view it would be far better if Central Park does not have a zoo rather than one that beguiles youngsters into the illogic that animals are like us. Regardless of what I think, however, this zoo is destined to fail. It will fail precisely because it isn't a zoo. That condition is apparent to any visitor. With the millions of tax-levied funds spent on this project, New Yorkers had every reason to expect more than they've received.

The problem as I see it is that the panjandrums who make decisions about such matters are far more affected by what is fashionably and politically acceptable than by what the public wants. Ask any kid if he'd prefer seeing a lion or a hamster. I'm reasonably sure of the answer. This zoo issue, like so many others facing New Yorkers, was determined without the benefit of common sense. It is hardly surprising that the result is such a disappointment.

The Central Park Zoo will be regarded as the manifestation of a denatured environment. That which is truly natural will have been converted into the artificial. At some point youngsters will have lost any connection with their primary ties to nature. Nature will be what appears in the Museum of Natural History or F. A. O. Schwartz. Wildness in nature, the uncivilized dimension, will be largely eviscerated from experience so that when on rare occasions it does arise, it will generate fear and loathing. This argument may seem like a rather exaggerated response to the Central Park Zoo, but the subtlety of the reformist effort knows no bounds. Now that the Central Park Zoo has been conquered, the Bronx Zoo may be next until children are convinced we are like animals and differences exist only as a figment of the imagination. At that moment humankind and the animal kingdom will have been disfigured beyond recognition.

September 28, 1988

7

Rauschenberg's Ego on Display

The Metropolitan Museum of Art's new wing of twentieth-century art—the Lila Acheson Wallace wing—is the home for Robert Rauschenberg's 10,000-square foot special exhibition space. "1/4 Mile or 2 Furlong Piece" is the American artist's continuing visual autobiography; it has a beginning but no end. Made up of undigested bits and pieces, image transfers, and recordings of sounds that caught the artist's fancy, this exhibit postulates the self-indulgent idea that art is the scrap heap analogue of one's memory. Here is unbridled solipsism at play, all the while disturbing because it is so innocent of guile.

Rauschenberg admits this is the personal collection of bits and pieces he has collected since the 1950s. A shirt here, a cardboard box there. There is certainly nothing in this collection that sets him apart from the rest of us. If there is an artistic vision—a matter I find most dubious—it may be found in his vanishing old cartons. Most of us simply throw them away.

In the center of the exhibit are three towers of books. These aren't the collected works of Robert Rauschenberg; they are works that hadn't been checked out of the Captiva library in ten years. "I gave them enough money to reinvest in the same number of brand new books," Rauschenberg noted. Why these books are a reflection of Rauschenberg's "visual autobiography" is a mystery. After all, by his own admission, these are not books he has read.

The rest of the exhibit purports to follow biographical events. But for those of us "unequipped" to evaluate Rauschenberg's aesthetic sensibility, it looks like a lot of junk attached to the wall. Of course, it is a lot of junk attached to the wall, but as Rauschenberg said, "Somebody's got to do it."

There are oil drums found on the highway, bricks taken from building sites, red tablecloths taken from a bar, stolen napkins, dirty laundry. Here is the flotsam and jetsam of thirty-five years of his life masquerading as an art form. If there is a talent on display, it is Mr. Rauschenberg's chutzpah, his immodest belief that his junk is art.

In order to justify this posing, Rauschenberg notes in the public description of his exhibit that it is devoted to "peaceful coexistence." How it is devoted to the promotion of peaceful coexistence isn't explained. It may well be that enemies of this nation will use this display of trash as yet another illustration of America's fall from cultural supremacy. However, the very reliance on "peaceful coexistence," as Rauschenberg's artistic vision is itself rather instructive.

When an artist has nothing to say; when he is bankrupt of ideas; when his "work" is little more than collecting the detritus of civilization, there is always that old standby to count on: peaceful coexistence. One wonders where Rauschenberg and many of his contemporaries would be without this old bromide. It is certainly convenient to have this handy cliché as a substitute for a well-developed artistic vision, or even as a substitute for real artistic work.

To his credit, Rauschenberg would probably be the first to admit that he is an artist using both meanings of the word. He is a put-on artist first and foremost. Most of what he says and much of what he does is with tongue in cheek. In fact, his tongue has been in his cheek so long there is a permanent protuberance on the side of his face.

However, it is not to the credit of the Metropolitan Museum of Art and its curators that they have devoted 10,000 square feet to Rauschenberg's egotistic escapade. In a century, appreciators of art will wonder why people came to a museum to observe junk instead of looking at their own garbage cans. It might very well be that many of the elitists who admire Rauschenberg have been so sheltered that they have never seen trash. For them, a soiled shirt or a carton may indeed be unusual.

Rauschenberg doesn't simply force us to observe the aesthetic in urban life, he forces us to observe the aesthetic in his life. This is little more than egotism on a canvass. From my point of view, it would be far more edifying to have a photograph of Rauschenberg framed and hung. As a matter of fact, the only fairly interesting picture in the exhibit is a photograph taken by Rauschenberg of a Crucifixion statue in a Chilean field. Rauschenberg probably thought of it as a self-portrait.

March 5, 1987

8

Historical Excision by New-Age Censors

There are simply no limits to the ideological fervor that can be marshaled by new-age prophets who use their own standards of right and wrong—feminist views being the prevailing model—to rewrite out history. Recently Claire Shulman, borough president of Queens in New York City, said she wants a large statue called "Civic Virtue" removed from its spot outside the Queens Borough Hall, where it has stood since 1941, because the "statue portrays women as evil and treacherous."

Now this is a rather curious characterization of a statue branded "civic virtue." The statue does depict a sword-bearing man, presumably representing civic virtue, triumphantly standing on mermaids, who are temptresses of vice and corruption. Since Queens is the borough that spawned Donald Manes and Geoffrey Lindinauer, well known for their corruption, Shulman does have a point. But the problem with her indignation is that it's misplaced.

It is hard to know if either the male or female figure or the mermaids stand for gender or mythology. If the latter, which seems plausible, it's hard to use her present sense of morality to banish the statue. In fairness to the borough president, she is not the first to criticize the "masculinity" of virtue and the "femininity" of vice, for others have made that claim since the statue was first unveiled in 1922. Nonetheless, the reason this issue is a cause célèbre has something to do with the *Zeitgeist*, not the statue.

So far down the slippery slope of ideological thinking have we gone that statues are evaluated on their conformity to a prescribed feminist position. I can imagine a women's group calling for the removal of the statue in front of the Vietnam memorial because it excludes women. Or perhaps even more absurd may be the call to raze the Washington Monument because it resembles a phallus.

Of course, there could be statues that so offend public taste that banishment is an appropriate response. A statue approving of the Holocaust or one admiring of the slave institution does not deserve public approbation. But does a statue depicting civic virtue involving a man and mermaids fall into this category?

So propagandized by feminist zeal are many people that one observer of the statue said, "I thought the man [in the statue] was the evil one because he's stepping on the women." I suspect that in a random selection of observers would be a disproportionate number who would share that observation. However, the real consideration in this analysis goes beyond the fate of a statue.

While it is always true that current histories tell more about the time in which they are written rather than the time about which they are written, it is not always true that a brand of wisdom intolerantly attempts to erase that portion of the past incompatible with its viewpoint. Yet the new-age prophets, who invariably point with pride to their tolerance, are actually intolerant enthusiasts of historical erasure. That which doesn't conform to their view of feminism and homosexuality is routinely subject to dismissal or, as is the case with the statue in question, banishment.

If these censors are successful in their efforts—Shulman is surely not alone in her campaign—a future generation will have only those public monuments that have passed a current political litmus test. What those proposing relocation or worse for some sculptures may actually accomplish is historical excision. Yet, however much we may excise the past, we cannot make the reality disappear. Systematic Soviet efforts to excise widespread starvation from its history have not been—in fact could not be—successful.

I suspect a similar fate awaits the "Civic Virtue" statue, despite Shulman's decision to have it banished. Those who do not share the borough president's sensibilities will ask what the fuss is about. Those who interpret the statue as a mythological statement will contend that Shulman has it all wrong. Those who value history will be appalled at this form of censorship. And those who are not bemused by this action will ask where it will ultimately end. But in fact the sentiments or motives of the artist—whatever they may be—can't be eliminated whatever attempts are made by the new-age censors to achieve this end.

December 8, 1987

9

Art Appears in an Unlikely Place

A visit to the museum has become a chore. No longer is the museum a place to wander through casually, stopping at a painting of choice; it is now an "educational center" with demanding and pretentious requirements. One is obliged to take instruction about the painters and their ideas as if in Fine Arts 101. With modern artists, most of whom are hucksters who produce more words than paintings—what Tom Wolfe has derisively called the *Painted Word*—the explanations are more important than the works.

These are artists who have retroactively developed a vision and purpose after putting several incomprehensible lines on a canvas. One must be told what the artist intended; intention is no longer determined by merely looking at a painting.

Museums now rent audio tapes, which offer a guided tour of predigested viewing with fifteen seconds spent in front of each masterpiece. Museum-goers are herded like cattle from one period to another as the narrator says, "It's time to leave the Middle Ages."

So grotesque is museum visiting for a generation obsessed with culture that it is not at all surprising that a different kind of museum has emerged in an unlikely setting, a setting where browsing is still possible and where knowledge about art isn't required. In some respects this is the ambience museums once had. Now, however, it is found almost exclusively in department stores at furniture exhibits.

A parlor, a library, and a bedroom are currently the focus of rooms with a Victorian view at Lord & Taylor in New York. Each room is decorated in the rich, warm Victorian style using authentic pieces or reproductions. Since the rooms were decorated by interior designers they have an appeal museum rooms rarely have. Museum curators contend the aesthetic is in the art object itself, not the way the art is presented—a view that usually detracts from the appreciation of art in a museum. I once heard a group of adolescents describe

Greek vases in the Metropolitan Museum of Art as "jelly jars being lined up for disposal." They had a point.

Bloomingdale's has staged a Mediterranean furniture display that features rooms from Morocco, Spain, Italy, France, Turkey, Greece, and Israel. The styles of the rooms vary in order to elicit the unique quality in each nation represented. Mr. Marvin Traub, the chairman of Bloomingdale's, described the rooms as "a symphony orchestra coming together." What he was getting at is the coherence and attention to detail that characterize such an exhibit. Here again coherence and detail are not usually qualities one finds in a museum exhibit, though they are common enough in department stores. Museum artifacts, when they are organized by room, successfully represent a period, even if the artists in that period had idiosyncratic and by no means compatible styles. In museums, in contrast, people are often heard wondering why certain paintings have been placed side by side.

Without going so far as to elevate department store displays into high culture—which would be to indulge in a kind of Andy Warhol inversion—it is possible to note that curators could learn a lot from these displays. For one thing, the presentation is often as important as the art itself. It's hard to appreciate a Cezanne so high on the wall one can hardly see it. Furniture displays are usually organized for coherence, a condition one rarely encounters in museums. But perhaps the single most important fact about department store displays is that they are designed for the browser. One doesn't have to be "prepared" for the experience.

There used to be a time when you could visit a museum on precisely these terms. This was the era before the fine-arts hype and the compulsion to "educate" the masses. Museums were places for contemplation. You could sit for hours, if you had the time and inclination, staring at a Tintoretto painting. Certainly the average museum visitor didn't have to worry about getting in the way of the stampede mobilized by audio recorders.

Unquestionably the times have changed. Museums are not what they were. But if you want solitude, a concern for detail, a lack of pretension, and a feeling that you can appreciate what you see without professional instruction, watch for special displays at your local department store.

December 10, 1987

10

Lamenting the Passing of the Old-Fashioned Neighborhood Schoolyard

This is a eulogy for a departed and sadly missed institution: the schoolyard. Like many other institutions in this city, including the trolley, the charlotte russe, Ebbets Field, it is only a memory of bygone days. That is not to suggest that schoolyards do not exist. They do. What has vanished is the institutional schoolyard—the place to meet one's friends, play basketball, compare notes on girls, test one's acumen on baseball statistics, and engage in debate with street-smart philosophers.

At the moment schoolyards don't even resemble their counterparts of the past. They are filled with rubble, marred with graffiti, and the people who meet there discuss coke and "horse" not hoops and "at bats." To play softball on one of these buckled diamonds is to test the limits of your ankle strength.

Yet I can remember a very different condition not so long ago. The schoolyard was a second home. I could learn about the mysteries of sex from world-weary braggadocios. I could hone my rebounding skills against 200-pound beer drinkers who systematically resisted the idea they might foul you. I could test my math prowess by carrying batting averages to the third decimal point during schoolyard one-upsmanship contests.

For example, in 1949 the National League batting champion, Jackie Robinson, and the two American League batting champions, George Kell and Ted Williams, finished with identical .342 averages. Days before the official declaration from the commissioners's office, my schoolyard colleagues and I computed the player with the highest average, George Kell.

There was an institutional bible. The *New York Post*. It was folded into quarters and put in your back pocket. Sports afficionados read it like the Old Testament from back to front. You read about sports achievements before you read about political failures. Very often you didn't get beyond the sports

21

pages. Out of habit I still read the paper this way and I memorize all the statistics that are listed as some arcane ritual associated with my past.

The schoolyard also allowed social intercourse to evolve without adult intervention. There weren't any coaches in the schoolyard. Little League games organized for kids by adults were as alien to the schoolyard experience as *New York Times* readers. This was a marketplace for talent. If Johnny couldn't hit a jump shot from fifteen feet, you didn't want him on your team. He might be a nice guy or even a friend; in the schoolyard only talent counted. This was an era before sociological arguments. You didn't worry about scarring someone's psyche. If he wasn't tough enough to accept the rules he didn't come to the schoolyard in the first place.

Another feature of this institution is that it resisted the constraints of time. One played in the schoolyard day and night. When darkness set in you played at the basket nearest the streetlight. Only when Dad came searching for you did the schoolyard day come to an end. It is interesting that Dad always knew where to find you. The days grew into seasons without any significant change in the schoolyard scene. What did change were the games. Stickball replaced basketball; softball replaced stickball; touch football replaced softball. If there was snow, you swept it away. If there was heat, you played in shorts and a tee shirt. The elements did not deter the schoolyard habitué.

Despite some of its positive features Mom would still say, "Why are you hanging around those schoolyard bums." It wasn't a question. She didn't know what the schoolyard was like; she relied on intuition. Today those schoolyard bums are professors, dentists, lawyers, deans, and a fair share of bums. Mom wasn't all wrong. Nonetheless, I lament the passing of this institution. The schoolyard was more than a place to spend some time. It was a place for nurturing; it was an educational arena.

If someone spoke of drugs in those days, you sent the person to a pharmacy. Sure, there were those who played cards and dice, but even that was in reasonable perspective. First, you showed your athletic talent, then you displayed the fast shuffle. The priorities were well established.

As I ride by a schoolyard littered with broken glass and empty of athletes, I think back to this institution when it was alive and well. It offered this city and its residents a great deal. Those like myself who profited from it are deeply saddened by its loss.

May 29, 1986

11

Winning the City Title:
Memory for a Lifetime

Thirty years ago this week, I realized the dream of every New York schoolboy athlete. My high school basketball team won the city championship. It was the only time in the history of Jamaica High School that this happened.

The game was played in Madison Square Garden in midmorning so that the basketball floor could be removed and the ice rink set up for a Ranger game that evening. Kids came pouring out of the subways carrying blue-and-red and black-and-gold pom-poms for their respective schools. We were playing against James Madison High of Brooklyn, a team with a strong basketball tradition and an outstanding center in Rudy La Russo, who later had a superb career at Dartmouth and with the Minneapolis and Los Angeles Lakers.

The Madison Square Garden marquee looked like shooting stars. Official school boosters for both sides started cheering an hour and a half before game time. Parents, aunts and uncles, and friends managed to overcome the stench of the elephants—the circus was in town—and found their seats. It was estimated that 17,000 people were at this game, making it a virtual sellout.

My coach, Charles Shannon, drove several of us to the arena. He was so anxious that three times he stopped at green lights. No one in the car pointed out the error. All of us had butterflies dancing in our stomachs.

The pregame discussion focused on two issues: how to counter the "box and one" defense we felt confident Madison would employ against our star, Alan Seiden, and what we would do to neutralize La Russo. However, my guess is that when the warm-ups began all the X's and O's faded into obscurity. This was Madison Square Garden, the place where Cousy and Schayes and Mikan plied their skills, and my team was playing for a prize coveted by every seventeen-year-old basketball player in the city.

Both teams began the game with turnovers. It was obvious that we paid a price for the butterflies. But when the players settled down, it proved to be a close game in which the skills of Seiden were clearly evident. When La Russo got into foul trouble in the second half, victory was within our grasp. At the final buzzer, boosters, fans, parents, and other relatives were on the court shouting congratulations for the city championship this Jamaica team had achieved, winning, 64–59.

I rarely see the guys from that team. The seniors were close to one another, but they treated juniors as upstarts who still had a lot to learn. I was one of three nonseniors on the squad. The following week, each player was given a championship sweater with one gold stripe on the left sleeve, an emblem proclaiming our victory, and a "J" for the school. That sweater gave me instant status on the blacktop basketball courts in this city. My Mom had to wash it when I was asleep. There was no other time when that sweater wasn't worn.

The memories of that day in March 1955 have faded, but they haven't vanished. It was a day for glory and growing up. The Madison Square Garden on 50th Street and Eighth Avenue is a parking lot. But when I pass that street I still see Jamaica High School boosters streaming out of the subway. I can still hear the chant of "J–A–M–A–I–C–A." I can still see a group of nervous guys with crewcuts warming up for the game.

The years pass quickly. But the other day I was reading about the chance another Queens team, Andrew Jackson High School, has to win the city crown today; I was reminded of thirty years ago. The city championship game is no longer played in Madison Square Garden (Jackson will play Kennedy at St. John's Alumni Hall). Yet the enthusiasm for the game hasn't waned.

If you think it has, ask a randomly selected adolescent carrying a basketball what he thinks about this city game. His smile will be the only answer you need.

March 17, 1985

12

Life on the Noisiest Street in Town

I live on the noisiest street in the world. There may be some who will be amused by this claim, but there is nothing amusing about it. Others may feel that they have stronger claims to live on the noisiest street.

But I believe from much experience that no street has the continuous din of Third Street between Mercer Street and La Guardia Place. There is never a respite; no one moment to relish sweet silence.

Some time between 3:30 and 5:30 A.M. oil deliveries begin for the New York University cogeneration facility. The deliveries occur every day including Saturday and Sunday. This is in clear violation of a city ordinance but the three companies in question, Triangle, Empire State, and Castle, don't care. The drivers want to avoid city traffic, so they deliver when it's convenient for them.

Police officials contend it's not their business to maintain the law, especially an ordinance as trivial as this one. So the practice continues. Between 5:30 and 6:30 A.M. the garbage trucks arrive. My garbage collector is a frustrated cymbal player. All his life he wanted to play for the New York Philharmonic at the moment during the "New World Symphony" when the crashing of percussion sounds awakens a new day. I have suggested that the sanitation authorities buy him a set of drums, but to no avail.

From 7:30 A.M. to noon the parade of vagrants seeking a meal at the Men's Shelter further east on Third Street begins. These unfortunate creatures, now called the homeless, are often mentally incompetent or drunk. Both conditions promote continual loud conversations to invisible companions. An occasional scream will emerge and an unseen adversary will be thrashed.

From noon till 6:00 P.M. Third Street is a major cross-street for trucks trying to get from the Williamsburg Bridge to the Holland Tunnel. Since Third Street widens between Mercer Street and La Guardia Place it is known to be an excellent alternative to the Houston Street route. No one bothered to tell these truck drivers that one side of Third Street has residential buildings. In any case, I doubt they would care.

At 6:00 P.M. university students and members of the community start jockeying for parking spaces. This is a daily ritual to avoid alternate-side-of-the-street parking restrictions. Once cars are in place and the streets darken, vandals break automobile windows in their search for booty, setting off alarms that ring through the night.

But these sirens are a mere trifle compared to the fire trucks stationed on both sides of Third Street. One extraordinary fact I've learned is that fires in lower Manhattan occur only between 2:00 and 4:00 A.M.

There is a correlation between the time I'm asleep, or should I say trying to sleep, and the time fires occur. Should one night pass without fire trucks—a rare occasion indeed—the oil trucks will be present to create the effect of life in a boiler room.

These are, of course, not the only sounds that set Third Street apart from its uptown competitors. Other streets are afflicted with radio blasters, jackhammers, water pumps, and construction gangs, but only Third Street is a drag strip for motorcyclists.

Some time between 2:00 and 5:00 A.M. three or four motorcyclists meet at Mercer Street. On a count of three they tear down Third Street at breakneck speed.

The only vehicle impeding the race is the oil truck making its delivery. The truck driver is bemused; there isn't much to do on Third Street at 4:00 A.M. Motorcycle-exhaust sounds rock through the night resembling mortar assaults in battle. Of course, this is a battle of a kind.

I watch this scene from my bedroom window wondering why this is happening to me. The last time I had a full night's sleep New York was buried under fifteen inches of snow. Until that happens again I'll stare at the scene on Third Street as my blood boils and the bags under my eyes grow deeper.

January 4, 1986

13

New York, New York, But Oh . . .

If one recalls that poignant scene in *Moscow on the Hudson* where the defector is apprehended in Bloomingdale's, the arresting officer says to someone holding the defector captive, "This is New York and in this city you do whatever you want."

Perhaps that is more true than either the police officer or the script writer imagined. In New York freedom is often defined as license.

Let me offer two illustrations. I often travel by cab from Greenwich Village to midtown along Park Avenue. At almost any hour of the day there is a traffic jam between 40th and 43rd streets as one enters the ramp around Grand Central Station.

The reason: Hyatt Hotel employees allow cars and trucks to double-park at the entrance so that three lanes are funneled into one. I have nothing against the Hyatt Hotel. In fact, its recent renovation is one I regard as most successful. I also believe that hotels should be accorded every opportunity to prosper in this city that relies heavily on tourism for its revenue.

But I don't understand how hotel employees and managers can arrogate to themselves control over a public thoroughfare. Moreover, I don't understand why the police don't do something.

A second illustration can be found in the defiance of dog owners who systematically violate the law. When the law first introduced fines against dog owners who do not clean up after their pups, there appeared to be police vigilance and public compliance. Now you have neither. Some dog owners have reverted to behavior as undisciplined as their pets. Their standard is if it doesn't move it can be used as a dog receptacle.

On my way to the subway the other morning, I observed a dog unable to control his biological calling in the middle of the street. I naïvely thought the owner would clean up the mess. Instead she simply kept on walking. As she approached me I stared at her, shaking my head in dismay. She looked at me and said in an angry voice: "You don't like it, you clean it up. This is as much my city as your city."

Indeed it is. In fact, self-defined freedom now impedes my path to the subway. But what can I do?

Albert Camus noted, "There is no justice, only limits." Surely he didn't have New York in mind. I often have the impression that the only limit on behavior is what you can get away with. A concern for one's neighbor is as anachronistic as giving up a seat to an elderly woman in a subway car.

Life goes on even when people selfishly ignore others. But we pay a price for it that is real and spiritual. If an ambulance can't get past the bottleneck on Park Avenue, a life may be at stake. If we accept dog excrement as a part of street life in this city, we can accept filth in any form.

Freedom without limits ultimately depreciates freedom.

November 16, 1985

14

New York's Lost Civility

Civility can't be measured like accidents on the highway or bank failures. Evidence of its decline is anecdotal. Nonetheless, I contend that anyone who can recall the last twenty-five years in this city has evidence of civility's decline.

I can remember when young people and occasionally adults were publicly admonished for littering or rowdiness. An elderly woman on the corner of my block used to watch me and my friends with a wary eye. When we were boisterous, she threatened to call our parents or have us declared nuisances. The threat usually worked.

So concerned was I that someone might see me throw a gum wrapper on the street that I stuffed the paper in my pocket.

When I started dating, I had the misfortune of falling for a girl who lived in the Bronx on 205th Street. I say misfortune because the trip from Queens was about the same traveling time on the subway as a flight from New York to Chicago. However, I made this trip with some regularity without a second thought.

As youngsters, we were told to help older people with their bundles from the grocery store. On one occasion, a woman gave me a tip. So appalled was my father that I had accepted this coin, he had me track down the woman and return the money.

I don't want to give the impression these deeds were done eagerly. My friends and I would have much preferred to play stickball or shoot hoops. But carrying a bundle was an obligation imposed by parents. We didn't have a choice in the matter. Recently the differences between my experiences then and experiences now came rushing to my thoughts when I told my adolescent daughter to avoid the subway in the late evening. Would you permit your child to ride unaccompanied from Queens to the Bronx? Most parents would prefer to have their children fish in the Gulf of Sidra.

Who in his right mind would admonish someone for littering? This infraction is considered trifling, hardly the kind on which one would stake his life. While there are still people who tell youngsters to "keep it down," noise is a ubiquitous feature of the city. Half the people on the streets are screaming at the other half or at the phantoms they see in the streets.

The only people I know who carry bundles are employed by the supermarket. Even as my groceries are delivered, a hand is outstretched for the tip. If someone would stop my wife on the street and volunteer to assist her with packages, my advice would be to keep walking.

Certainly this evidence is not conclusive. On balance, however, I am firmly convinced civility is in decline. If this seems like an exaggeration, randomly choose a youngster to assist you with your bundles. You don't have to report on the response. Anyone living in New York has already heard it.

May 9, 1986

15

Why Life in New York Is So Harsh

For a considerable period before Ed Koch's arrival on the scene, New York was afflicted by politicians whose soft-headed policies brought the city to the brink of bankruptcy and, by overly generous welfare payments, swelled the ranks of the poor.

From the pinnacle of its prestige after World War II, New York slid down the slope of fiscal irresponsibility and chaos in the '60s and '70s.

It was not uncommon in those decades for people to say, "New York is ungovernable." But probably no city would have been governable under the policies then in vogue here.

There are signs that the '80s will be viewed by city historians as a period of recovery. While the fiscal situation is not robust, neither is it on the brink of disaster. The unemployment rate hovers around 7 percent, or close to the national average. Crime statistics are declining, though some law-enforcement officials maintain that these numbers reflect reporting deficiencies. In the midst of these mostly favorable developments, there is one area in which the city has continued to decline.

Public barbarism—in the form of unruliness, a lack of manners, abusive language, and general disorder—is increasingly common. Roger Starr, in his marvelous book *The Rise and Fall of New York City*, attributes this moral decline to a failure of the city's "elites."

Prior to the '60s, leaders across the community insisted on conformity to reasonable standards of civil behavior. It was not just a matter of authority imposed by the police. Civilized conduct was perceived and generally accepted as a public duty. Teachers, counselors, social workers, and businessmen directed those who had been untrained and undisciplined into responsible behavior.

The results were not perfect, but they were good enough to create a tangible atmosphere of civic virtue. When in the '60s the dominant groups lost confidence in traditional values or became skeptical of their importance, the guidance needed to sustain social control was undermined. If the middle class didn't believe in its own established rules of behavior, why should those in the lower stratum?

The disdain for personal responsibility that has always been the mark of the undisciplined became, ironically, the model for leaders lacking confidence in their own tradition. Personal blame for antisocial behavior was replaced by "society's fault." Illustrations of this antimiddle-class attitude abound. Kids smoke in the subway in defiance of the law. Relatively few people cover their mouths when coughing in a public place. Middle-class women talk like sailors in a bar. People push while getting on and off buses.

The phrase "excuse me" has become archaic. Radios are used as an assault mechanism by self-absorbed adolescents. Rarely do youngsters give up a seat on the subway for the elderly. In the age of egalitarianism, everyone must fend for himself. Public places have become the preserve of thugs, except where the police are constantly vigilant.

Thus, despite all the political and economic improvements one can cite, New Yorkers live in an increasingly uncivilized environment. Unless we revive and enforce a code of decent behavior for our social contacts, we shall continue to feel assaulted and threatened.

The businessmen with a $100,000 salary, the elderly on Social Security, and the welfare recipient are all trapped in the social anarchy caused by the abandonment of traditional norms and values. It isn't easy to prescribe remedies for this problem. But no solution is possible without leadership, and that leadership must emerge from the sectors of society that abdicated that responsibility more than a decade ago. Without that guidance New York will remain a harsh place in which to live.

If the mayor is really interested in how he's doing, he should spend more time on this difficult issue.

October 30, 1985

16

Radical Chic Pervades Ritzy Parties
on Park Avenue

Once I was invited to one of those chic Park Avenue parties, the kind where the canapés are presented with a French accent. In attendance were a physician, his social-worker wife, a businessman, his buoyant, much younger student wife, and my wife and I. On the face of it this should have been one of those boring dinners where pleasantries are exchanged and you keep praying the second-hand on the clock will ignore the constraints of time so you can say goodbye without embarrassment. This unfortunately was not to be.

What I heard during this party did not come off the pages of an Irving Kristol exegesis on the new class, nor was it a sociological dissection of the upwardly mobile, liberally oriented snobbish view of reality that is the calling card of the baby-boomers. Here was radical chic in all its glory.

The physician, who sprinkles French idioms in his conversation the way I put pepper on scrambled eggs, said: "I care only about the extension of life. Nothing else makes any difference. Religion, after all, is the opiate of the masses."

I hastened to reply that while I approve of life extension, I am equally interested in how lives are lived. "This brings one willy-nilly to religion," I said.

"How trite!" he mocked scornfully.

At dinner the businessman's wife waxed lyrical about her study of history until she came to a discordant note: "There was *real* art in the past and literature, but, after all, we didn't have a women's movement."

"Perhaps," I rejoined, "women in the past didn't need one."

"My, you are a funny man" she responded, dismissing me. Her husband, swept up in conversation about Latin America, said our policies are myopic. "We should embrace the radicals down there who express the will of the discontented masses."

"How do we know," I inquired, "that those radical leaders, who invariably come from the wealthiest groups, represent the masses?"

"Oh that's just axiomatic," he replied condescendingly.

The first course was a fish mousse that would be easy for a toothless woman to digest, but I couldn't swallow mine. Noticing my inability to eat and by now conspicuous silence, the doctor volunteered: "Isn't New York wonderful! When I was recently in Los Angeles a colleague asked me why I didn't move out there. I said there are three reasons and they all begin with New York: *New York Times, New Yorker, and New York Review of Books.*"

My peristalsis was now moving in the wrong direction. There are many reasons to love New York, starting with the Battery and moving up to Grant's Tomb. But I never once, in my many years of being domiciled here, thought of these three journals as the reason for staying. In fact, I've often thought this is what New Yorkers have to overcome like traffic jams and surly cabbies. Now I'm told this is the New York contribution. These suspiciously pretentious and unusually misguided avatars of public taste are being presented as New York's contribution to the world.

No wonder this doctor said "Merci" instead of "Thank you" after every course. No wonder God is dead for him; He was killed on the pages of the the *New York Review*. No wonder life extension is all that counts when values are systematically betrayed by partners in almost every story printed in the *New Yorker*.

It was bitterly cold that evening as we left the party together, each couple in desperate search for a cab. As luck would have it my wife and I found one first. On the way downtown we passed the doctor and his wife still eagerly remonstrating for a taxi. I rolled my window down and said, "C'est dommage, or in New Yorkese, up yours." Somehow I don't think we'll be seeing them again soon, but who cares. In their eyes I am a boor; in mine, they are the supercilious snobs who are part of our national problem.

Maybe the next time—if there is a next time—I shall go to one of these parties dressed like a sanitation worker. Since the new class purports to sympathize with the poor between courses of fish mousse and chicken breasts in Cointreau, how can I be rejected?

July 27, 1984

17

There's More to Being a WASP Than Money: Most Are Really Only Waspy

There are words that enter common parlance whose meaning has been thoroughly perverted by misuse. In fact what happens is that the continually misused version is what is widely perceived as accurate. One such illustration is the expression *hoi polloi*, which means the common people. However, every time I hear this phrase employed it is in reference to some elite group. The other day a cab driver referred to a diamond-clad, fur-draped woman as *hoi polloi*. Now he may know something about her I do not, but I suspect the words were used improperly. I've discovered that this misuse occurs so often that *hoi polloi* has come to assume its opposite meaning.

Perhaps the most interesting illustration of this kind is the acronym WASP. Surely most people know that WASP stands for White Anglo-Saxon Protestant. However, ethnics invariably use the expression to refer to anyone of wealth and stature. Since New York is a town of ethnics, WASP has a special meaning here; the word has been apotheosized to suggest a special meaning, namely, elegance, well attired, snobbish, noblesse oblige. I recently heard an elderly Jewish woman refer to stores on Madison Avenue as "waspy." Now it is true these stores are elegant, but they are distinctly non-WASP. Most are owned by Italian and French proprietors.

Surely, there are WASPs who are "waspy." The quintessential example is John Lindsay. He is tall, thin, Ivy-educated, elegant, tanned, and has the "right" hairstyle. Moreover, even though he lives in New York he acts as if he'd choke on a knish and suffer pangs of indigestion after eating pizza. However, it is important to distinguish between a WASP and what is now called waspy.

Most WASPs aren't waspy. In fact, most WASPs are poor and middle class. Appalachia is filled with WASPs, yet no one ever thought of calling these people waspy. The word has been so transmogrified that non-WASPs desperately want to be waspy. One woman I know with a decidedly ethnic appearance to her nose, said to her plastic surgeon, "Please make mine waspy."

Of course, WASP can be a form of derision as is the case when people say, "You eat like a WASP." What they may mean is that you eat very little. But it may also mean that one prefers watercress sandwiches or finger sandwiches without crust or would prefer to drink a lunch in the form of a dry martini. There is no evidence, of course, that WASPs drink more than the Irish. In fact, since whiskey is high in calories it is a decidely unwaspy drink.

What has happened is that accuracy of meaning has been lost in the swelter of misusage. I have a friend who is so appalled by the inaccurate use of WASP that when he wants to describe what many now call waspy, he refers to an E. This translates into an eastern, establishment Episcopalian. He may be onto something. If one distinguishes between Protestant sects by saying, "A Methodist is a Baptist with shoes, a Presbyterian is a Methodist with a college degree, and an Episcopalian is a Presbyterian with a seat on the stock exchange," then E could be a fine addition to colloquial language.

But I don't think it can possibly catch on. First of all, Episcopalians won't cooperate. Those of them who have wealth are uncomfortable with it. The sermons in Episcopal churches are often about identifying with our poor brothers someplace or other. This is the first sign that they may be losing their waspiness. Second, so many of the ministers look and talk as if they are plain folk that most of us may start to believe that. And third, the Episcopal origins in England are beclouded by a past that is distinctly unwaspy. The more the brethren know about their church the more difficult it will be to keep elitism intact.

What then are we to do about such terminology? Obviously, the overuse of WASP suggests there is a need for such a word. Many substitutes are possible, such as the "Park Avenue Pretentious." But the acronym PAP would only cause problems for gynecologists. There is the ever popular "snob," but that is employed as a pejorative and lacks the positive qualities of "waspy." My recommendation is that we keep waspy and try to unhinge it from its parental WASP. This won't be easy to do. But then again, there are so few true-blue WASPs left in New York that before long there will be many who are waspy, and few who are WASP.

June 4, 1985

18

"About Men" Is Really about the New Age

It seems to me about time that someone put the swarmy self-confessionals in the "About Men" columns of the *New York Times* into perspective. Each week men bare their souls for the presumptive edification of readers. There is also at work the catharsis so evident in a culture obsessed with "getting it all out."

Yet "About Men" is actually about only one kind of man. The one who is routinely featured invariably mocks the macho image. This male cries at movies, has recently discovered the joys of household work, has heart-to-heart discussions with his children in which his errors in child-rearing are explained, and prefers cooperation to competition. Were they not so predictable and insidious, these articles would be laughable. However, it's hard to laugh when you realize this column is devoted to cultural assault.

Let me illustrate with a recent article entitled "The Art of Losing" by Michael Blumenthal, a poetry instructor at Harvard and psychotherapist in Cambridge. Blumenthal contends that the message of male nurturing is competition in which winning is everything: "One man's triumph always entails another man's defeat." Now, however, Blumenthal proclaims his fatigue with being that kind of man; he can't wait to tell his girlfriend that he isn't ashamed to lose. Goodbye competition, so long to the pursuit of teaching at Harvard and "scoring" with women. Here is the new, healthy American male.

What Blumenthal neglects to reconcile is that he does teach at Harvard. One might also ask what aspirations had to be pursued to get his piece published in the *New York Times*. One might also ask if the new, vulnerable Blumenthal—the one challenging the male psyche—isn't espousing a new line for his gullible female friends. Clearly the road to masculinity includes many of the features that Blumenthal cites. It also includes many of the features Blumenthal denies. Most men I know unselfconsciously clean their homes, do the dishes, and cry when they are moved. They simply don't write articles proclaiming their sensitivity.

This article, like so many of its predecessors, relies on the admission that men would be better off if they didn't compete. After all, it is usually noted, everyone can't win. Alas, that is true. But winning and competing are not the same. The desire to achieve in our society is fostered by the dream of winning. Young males—until recently—have grown up with the canon of life: to achieve one must be capable of competing. There aren't victories to cite in middle age, but what one finds is the urge to achieve.

That there is a downside to this achievement orientation is undeniable, but on balance the achievement model has done more to promote wealth and social justice than all the bland assertions for demasculinization that appear on the pages of the *New York Times* and in the new-age quarterlies that welcome the "I'm okay, you're okay, we're okay and there are no winners in this society" line of argument.

Recently David Holaman, writing in the *New York Times*, indicated that the emphasis on winning in athletics, most notably in the Olympics, is wrongheaded. According to him the games "are supposed to be a diversion, a sidelight to life, not the business we pursue and promote gravely and with excessive flag waving." It may be of interest to Holaman that sports are not a "sidelight to life." They are important precisely because they encourage the competition that translates into achievement. Moreover, the lure of the gold in the Olympics is what inspires athletes to put out their best effort, to go beyond their capabilities. Michael Novak understands the matter properly, I believe, by noting that American athletes at the Olympics seemed to be content with sixth-place finishes that were an improvement on their tenth-place aspirations.

Insinuating itself into our culture are the beliefs that winning doesn't matter and competition is bad. It is not entirely coincidental that many Americans are no longer willing to defend national interests and believe there isn't any justifiable reason for going to war. There is the widely held cliché that everyone has something to offer and, as a consequence, judgments about people are inappropriate. There is the contagion of undifferentiated grades in our schools. There is the myth that everyone is handicapped. There is the psychology that competition makes us neurotic; that winning is an obsession with deleterious cultural effects.

With this view in the ascendancy, this nation rarely wins the gold at the Olympics, finds it difficult to compete with Japanese trade, has observed a deterioration in the quality of its education, rationalizes Soviet military adventurism in its own hemisphere, and organizes social policy for exceptional cases instead of the average person in the hope that equity will be achieved. While the "About Men" column can't possibly be associated directly with these issues, there isn't any question that the view propounded is consistent with an egalitarian utopia in which achievement and excellence are relegated to the ashheap of history.

March 22, 1988

19

Renovating the Lower East Side
of Our Imagination

For years the Lower East Side was a shrine. Jews from all over Europe who migrated to the United States and once lived in this neighborhood would return on Sundays to soak up memories of days gone by. Only on Delancey Street could one find a truly sour pickle from a barrel. The best bargains in town were to be found on Allen Street. And Orchard Street was New York's ultimate fleamarket.

But the signs of social malaise struck this neighborhood in the 1960s. Junkies shot up dope in the basements of abandoned buildings; prostitutes were on every street corner; crime ruled the streets. As much as Jews felt drawn to the old neighborhood, many were afraid to come.

Of course there are lures. Ratner's still has a mushroom-barley soup that sets off gastronomic pleasure rarely encountered in fancy uptown restaurants. You can still make an egg cream at your own table in Sammy's Roumanian, and Fein and Klein has knock-off prices on leather bags that have women smiling with self-satisfaction. But it's not the same as it once was. Although this area is ripe for development in a town desperate for new residences, the lower East Side is virtually ignored.

A five-block area bounded by Delancey, Norfolk, Grand, and Clinton streets lies vacant. There have been plans for development, but the community board obsessed with "low-cost housing" puts a monkey wrench in the plans. That there are many low-cost projects in the area—in fact more low-cost housing than in any Manhattan neighborhood—doesn't seem to make the slightest difference.

The East Side Chamber of Commerce and some community groups have argued that this parcel of land be sold at public auction and part of the proceeds earmarked for low-cost housing in an obvious attempt to mollify the community board. In order to ensure fair bidding on this land, there should be no constraints imposed other than construction that is compatible with the zoning regulations.

It's difficult to know whether this kind of development scheme could make a difference in a neighborhood suffering from decades of decay. Then again it might be a catalyst for other development. After all, the location is ideal.

From Delancey and Clinton streets you can get to La Guardia Airport in fifteen minutes. You can take a subway to midtown in minutes. And you can walk across the street and gorge yourself on Ratner's mushroom-barley soup.

Admittedly, those new buildings might change one's memories of yesteryear. It's true the spirit of the old Delancey Street is not easily recaptured. Rapaport's is gone forever, as is the old hawker and his pickle barrel on the corner of Essex. Kids don't play stickball in the streets. Peddlers don't sell from pushcarts. The world has changed. But from my point of view it is better to have development that is different than decay that is permanent and inexorable. At the moment the empty lots and broken-down buildings are staging areas for crime. I don't see how that helps anyone but the criminal.

Nostalgia in this instance could be a powerful force for redevelopment. Women wearing white gloves and fur coats might once again parade up and down Delancey Street. Perhaps a steak restaurant will open in the old Rapaport's site. Maybe Sammy can be convinced to relocate. Nightclubs might echo with Yiddish tunes. The old Essex Market could open, selling gefilte fish, pickled herring, lox and bagels.

A community resurgence is certainly not out of the question. Stranger things have happened. Who would have predicted twenty years ago that Columbus Avenue would become New York's Via Veneto? Delancey Street is distinctly New York; it resonates with the sounds of this city. Captive in the walls of old tenement buildings are the cries of a newly arrived people in this extraordinary metropolis. Wherever there are New Yorkers who care about their past, there should be New Yorkers who care about this neighborhood.

Let the old stoops come alive. Give vitality to a neighborhood in the doldrums. Delancey Street should be a working museum; a South Street Seaport with memories of the immigrant experience. If the community board members don't have that vision, then the politicians should impose it on them. New York deserves a revivified East Side. New York's children deserve a chance to share the memories.

November 20, 1986

Part II

Politics

20

The Cable TV Fiasco

Why is it that millions of American city dwellers are in the last frontier for cable television? This question becomes striking when one considers the small towns and suburban areas that have had cable stations for fifteen and twenty years, while the nation's largest cities are still waiting—and will probably keep waiting for another five years—for cable wires to reach their homes.

The answer to the question is apparent to anyone living in a metropolitan area: politics. It isn't *any* politics to which I'm referring; it's big-city socialist politics. In the major cities where cable wire has not yet been laid there are enormous arguments over who should build the system and who gets the franchise. The franchise agreements recently signed for Brooklyn and the Bronx in New York City culminated a process that began in the 1960s. This two-decade negotiation has been punctuated by bribery, corruption, dirty-dealing, and politics of the most Byzantine variety.

About 745,000 miles of cable wire now criss-cross the nation—making cable television available to 70 million homes, or about 80 percent of the nation's people. Almost all of the unwired 20 percent of the country are in urban areas.

In New York City large portions of Queens, Brooklyn, and the Bronx are not yet hooked up. In Cleveland the franchise contract was signed in 1986 and most homes will be wired in three years. In Washington D.C. 17,000 of the city's 254,000 homes were wired this year. Discussion about cable began in that city in 1975. In Baltimore construction started in 1985 and cable now reaches about 17 percent of the city's homes. In Philadelphia about a quarter of the city's homes can obtain cable. The city awarded contracts to six cable companies in 1966, but the system wasn't built due to regulatory problems. In Detroit construction began a year ago and cable is available for a quarter of the city's homes. In Chicago 75 percent of the city is wired, but the contracts for full wiring were negotiated in the late 1960s.

What this status report indicates is that in the nation's largest cities decades of negotiation transpired before a cable system was put in place. This negotiation has involved some of the most bitter exchanges since Boss Tweed organized Tammany Hall, for at the end of this cable rainbow is a pot of gold filled to overflowing.

Yet in the last analysis it is not greed and corruption that stifled the construction of cable wiring in urban areas, but a government made impotent by layers of bureaucracy and coruscating regulations. One might be opposed to corruption on moral grounds, but, if anything, payoffs should have greased the wheel of construction, making cable TV a reality in urban areas long before now. The fact that small towns and suburban areas had cable for twenty years suggests that if you want to get something done in the United States avoid cities stifled by the weight of their bureaucratic organizations.

That bureaucracy exists in major urban areas is not explained only by their sheer size. In most cases bureaucracy is a reflection of a philosophical penchant. The liberal administrations in the major cities used bureaucracy as camouflage for their political goals. Bloated bureaucracies are part of a patronage system. Regulatory statutes are a way of appeasing special-interest groups. Decelerating the construction of projects enhances political payoffs. Not one of the cities mentioned in this article has been untainted by payoffs related to cable installation.

But my view is not intended to be moralistic. If I were to dig I'm sure similar examples of payoffs could be found in small towns. However, the difference between small towns and big cities is in the nature of their political organizations. As the twentieth century has demonstrated time and time again, socialism is incapable of producing results because it is unresponsive to market conditions.

If big cities could unshackle themselves from the crushing condition of socialist views that now prevail, they might yet be places congenial for salubrious living. However, the power of gerrymandering has made almost every major U.S. city a Democratic enclave and in the process a lumbering and inefficient entity for social organization. If that seems like hyperbole, ask yourself why Scottsdale, Arizona, has had cable for twenty years while most of the residents of Brooklyn, New York, don't have it today.

January 14, 1988

21

Why Politicians Misunderstand Problems

Two letters to the *New York Times* display in the most graphic form the disparity between what is known by scientists and what is believed and acted on by politicians. One of the authors is an archaeologist who digs into modern landfills for information about garbage. After painstakingly sorting our trash, this fellow discovered that fast-food packaging—the latest culprit in the environmental war—accounts for ".26 percent by weight, .27 percent by volume" of the landfills excavated. Naturally he points out, there is some variability, "but less than one-third of 1 percent was fast-food packaging of all kinds. . . ."

The other letter writer, a New York City Council member, indicates that he "submitted bills to prohibit chlorofluorocarbon processed food packaging and to impose a tax on plastic and other containers to encourage recycling." His argument for this legislative action is the prevention of landfill degradation. Moreover, he even admonishes against the purchase of plastic packaging by the city and its use at any city-sponsored event.

While scientists do not always provide incontrovertible evidence, my guess is that an archaeologist who sorts, screens, and measures garbage is better prepared to evaluate its content than a politician whose only contact with garbage is in a can next to his home or in discussion at the city council. Nonetheless, the politician invokes the fierce-sounding consequence of "landfill degradation" if his warning isn't heeded. Perhaps less than one-third of 1 percent of a landfill can make a difference, but logic would dictate that so small a percentage of plastic in a landfill is not a matter over which to rant.

Yet in the political vineyards of this era several conditions are at work. A politician doesn't really have to know very much in order to take a stand. There are those infused with ideological ardor who are prepared to defend their "courageous position" in the struggle against you name it—profligate

45

capitalists, indiscriminate dumpers, get-rich-quick artists, or anyone who doesn't share the epiphanies of current fashion.

A politician does have to demonstrate that one's heart is in the right place. That place has been preempted by a utopian agenda that includes environmental purity, risk aversion, and an antipathy to development and new technology. When I told the director of a major philanthropy that his devotion to environmental purity perils development and is unquestionably a political stand, he replied, "My view of nature has nothing to do with politics; I offer you a humanitarian position." In the new age, markets that produce efficiencies are a reflection of a political ideology, while those who wish to dictate land use are humanitarian.

A politician needs an issue; it's what gives a politician visibility. He or she must be known as a sponsor of some bill whether that bill entails needed reform or not. That free societies are composed of competing interests with every legislator in the business of adopt-a-cause means, in effect, that either taxes must inevitably rise, a debt must be expected, or the bank will go bust. At the moment legislators are far more interested in a personal cause to launch careers than some transcendent idea of public welfare, even though their legislative bills invariably elicit claims of the public good.

This landfill illustration can be duplicated in hundreds of cases. In fact it would be useful to compare what is known about an issue like acid rain and the legislation that was introduced to eliminate the problem. In most instances a legislative effort to solve a problem results in throwing billions of dollars at a million-dollar issue. The attempt to elevate health care into a political issue fixed by the beneficence of legislators has led in the end to spiraling health costs that are widely regarded as out of control.

It may well be that chlorofluorcarbons in our landfills pose some danger of arguable proportions. In the hands of a legislator, however, the danger will be blown out of proportion, the expense to the taxpayer will be larger than the issue warrants, the contents of the bill will not resemble the known characteristics of the problems and, in the end, only the legislative sponsor will benefit from the political activity.

February 18, 1988

22

The New Dictators of the Department of Environmental Conservation

Zygmont Maslowski came to this country twenty-seven years ago from his native land of Hungary. He is an ardent foe of communist role, knowing firsthand how such regimes operate. When Maslowski arrived in the United State penniless he began working seven days a week, sixteen hours a day, with one purpose in mind: buying a home for his wife and children. At a public auction he bought a parcel of land in Staten Island, using all of his savings. This was to be his dream home in the land of the free for his wife and three children, ranging in age from eleven to twenty-eight.

One year after buying this land, Maslowski received a letter from the Department of Environmental Conservation (DEC; a New York State agency) telling him his property was a designated wetland and as such could not be "altered." Barbara Rinaldi, regional permit administrator of the DEC, wrote: "Enclosed with this notice [that your property is on a wetland] is a brief description of the Freshwater Wetlands Act and how it affects wetland owners." How it actually would affect homeowners in this so-called wetland region was a matter unknown to everyone including employees of the DEC. A local Staten Island bank decided not to provide a mortgage for any home that is in a designated wetland region. The Maslowskis found themselves in Catch-22 New York style.

Through government fiat Maslowski's property was usurped. All his hard-earned money was in effect sequestered. There was no hearing, no trial, no compensation. The panjandrums sitting in the Region Two office of the DEC had acted. When I asked Maslowski about this decision he replied with a question: "How is this system different from communist Hungary? In Hungary," he noted, "innocent people and honest people don't have choices. Here the same is true. I put my life on the line for a home, now I have nothing."

Zygmont Maslowski is not alone. Isabel and Vito Basile bought an old barn

47

in Staten Island with the object of renovating the structure as their home. But when their property was designated as a wetland the appraised value was cut in half by the bank carrying the mortgage and an amendment was added to the Basiles loan based on the wetland judgment.

So rigidly applied is the wetlands designation that the dried brush outside the Basile home can't be cut during the dry summer months when such flora acts as kindling. There have been times when the Basiles and their four children have abandoned their home for fear of the fire hazard. Old cars and debris are routinely thrown in the so-called wetlands area. But when the Basiles have called the Sanitation Department to have the junk removed, they were told sanitation equipment isn't permitted on wetlands property. Presumably the removal of garbage isn't environmentally sound.

The widening of a narrow road that had been the site of numerous automobile collisions in Staten Island came to a standstill when the DEC claimed that a portion of the expanded highway is on freshwater wetlands. Wayne Richter, a biologist with the state agency, said "the plans call for too much encroachment on state-protected wetlands." Assistant City Transportation Commissioner John McTigue, in a sharp exchange with Richter, argued, "What good are wetlands if people are being killed?"

Governor Mario Cuomo finally said a committee representing all interests would be empowered to consider the problem. Overlooked in the governor's decision, however, is the arbitrary way in which the DEC conducts its business. According to the agency report a wetland is any area in which trees or vegetation survive that may ordinarily be found in a wetland. Yet there isn't any information on specific parcels. As Marc Gerstman, director of the Legal Affairs Division of the DEC noted, "The Department as required by the Act, has studied and mapped the areas subject to regulation on a wetland system basis. Voluminous files exist pertaining to these systems and will be relied on in defense of designations. Information that is specific to particular tax blocks and lots is available in some cases." However, the voluminous files do not address specific cases, notwithstanding the claim that such information is available in some instances.

In fact a "wetland" is what the DEC calls a wetland. This tautology has been elevated into an environmental defense. The fact that the red maple, weeping willow, and red gum trees can be found in "dry" soil doesn't seem to affect the wizards of environmental purity working for the state.

What troubles me even more than the agency position is that honest, hard-working people seeking a modest place in the sun are considered less important than the survival of a red maple tree. One doesn't have to be opposed to environmental positions to recognize the absurdity in this DEC stand. Environmentalism has become the new religion. Instead of a balanced approach to nature in which the interests of people are weighed against possible environmental damage, there is the emergence of an orthodoxy that cannot tolerate any challenge to purity.

Lost in the swelter of defensive agency rhetoric is the condition of a disheartened Hungarian convinced that this nation is not different from his homeland and a family embittered by the constant fear that its home will be burned to the ground. Who can blame these people for being dismayed? Why is a governor, who gives speeches about the "national family," so unresponsive to the families in his own state and city that desperately need a helping hand? Why is the Department of Environmental Conservation more concerned about the survival of a species of tree than the survival of families whose taxes pay their salaries? Perhaps the state hearing in January, which will consider this wetlands issue, will have answers to these questions. However, like the many residents of Staten Island, I'm skeptical.

December 28, 1987

23

The Byzantine Politics of New York

A friend of mine knowledgeable about city politics described for my edification the difference between New York's parties. As he put it, the difference between Republicans and Democrats is the firms that get government contracts. In fact ideology and policy—the matters on which I thought politics rest—are irrelevant.

On reflection this description makes a lot of sense. Some time in the 1960s public service as a calling came to an end in this city. One didn't take a municipal job to improve urban life; one recognized that there was a pot of gold that could be dispensed to help one's friends and party associates. Politics became a business. Not all of this business is technically corrupt, albeit soft money breeds corruption. But the winners in an election dispense favors in the form of contracts to a host of well-heeled city panjandrums, including those in real estate, law, public relations, communications, journalism, garbage collection, et al.

The goal in New York politics is victory. Everything else, including improvement of city life, is beside the point. If this seems like a jaded view, consider the well-publicized corruption in the parking bureau, taxi commission, Wedtech, and dozens of other examples. However, what is undisclosed is equally poignant. The power wielded by law firms and real estate interests in getting people elected and in securing contracts for services rendered from the newly installed city administration is the proverbial grease in the machine.

This characterization is not designed to point fingers or declare illegality. It is perfectly legal to insist that a law firm get a contract with the city in return for political support. Whether it is ethical or not is another question. That Victor Gotbaum's son is working for Felix Rohatyn, who sits on the Municipal Assistance Corporation (MAC) board, is hardly surprising. That the governor's son can wield enormous power from his recent law office appointment, with minimal experience, is not a statement about his natural endow-

51

ments, however extraordinary they may be. That Andrew Stein's father is treasurer of the New York State Democratic party is not coincidental.

Those people who march behind candidates in a campaign believe that ideas matter. That's usually why they volunteer their time during a campaign. But in New York, politics is the business of the municipal pork barrel. Those who give, get. The team that wins selects its friends to do the work of the city. Among the insiders this is described as "getting contracts." At the moment it is also a description of city politics.

Can this system be broken? My answer it equivocal. As long as tax-levied funds are perceived as a pork barrel to be dispensed by the winners to their supporters, change is unlikely. As long as ideas are the enemy of politics, change is unlikely. As long as law firms don't have to engage in full disclosure about their city contracts, change is unlikely. As long as New York has what is tantamount to a one-party system, change is unlikely.

However, with corruption clearly exposed, there is scarcely a New Yorker unaware of political conditions in this town. The morality of public service may not be the same now as when John Adams described it at the end of the eighteenth century, but there are decent, independent people in this town who can't be bought and who wish to serve their fellow New Yorkers. Whether they can get elected is another matter.

New York is an unusual place in that it is bigger, more extreme, more wonderful, more difficult than any other place in the world. It's politics are also more Byzantine than in any other place in the world. Despite its size there are probably fewer power brokers in New York than in Indianapolis. There is more to be gained with little risk than almost any other place in the free world. New York is a place to do business, to shop, to write books. People don't come here to engage in politics.

In part that explains why the political game has been left to a few who are dedicated to keeping it that way. Since most New Yorkers vote along ethnic lines with scarcely a second look at their candidates, we tend to get the officers we deserve. But, it seems to me, it's time to disclose what is actually going on here. This is Vince Lombardi's city in a real sense: winning is everything. Politics is dispensing favors; people who have other ideas about public office should either move to another place or try to reform the system. The former can be discouraging and the latter isn't easy, but these are the alternatives. As Frank Sinatra said, "If you can make it there, you can make it anywhere." Sinatra may not have been referring to New York politics, but then again, perhaps he was.

June 4, 1987

24

A Black Cop Rejects "Quota" Promotion

Samuel Brown, a fourteen-year veteran of the New York City Police Department, passed up a promotion and a concomitant $7,000-a-year raise because, he said, it "was unearned." He contends it wasn't a difficult decision because the reason for the promotion was racial and "I just don't believe in racial quotas."

Brown, assigned to the Queens Patrol Borough Task Force, was one of the v765 cops offered promotion after a court-ordered settlement over the 1983 sergeants' test. According to the racial quotas mandated by the court, those promoted included ninety-four blacks, eighty-nine with scores below the passing grade, and sixty-six Hispanics, thirty-four with scores below the passing grade. Brown scored higher than the 65.3 percent cutoff grade for blacks, but lower than the 79.2 percent minimum score required of whites.

For him the decision was a matter of conscience. A colleague noted, "Brown did not want to be marked as a quota cop." After fourteen years, Brown obviously feels he is as qualified to be a sergeant as any white cop. But he will not take the job based on mandated affirmative-action criteria. He has decided to take the exam again until he passes.

Roger Abel, president of the 2,500-member Guardians Association, which represents black patrolmen, detectives, and superior officers, said, "Everybody tried to talk him into taking it." It also appears that officials in the Police Department urged Brown to take the promotion. But he could not be dissuaded. Abel noted further that "He [Samuel Brown] can't get higher standards by rejecting something he's entitled to—the courts made a decision that there was something wrong with the instrument and consequently, we got redress [sic]."

While it is certainly true that the courts have responded to complaints about the civil service exam, it is also true that the courts have been under enormous political pressure to mandate affirmative-action plans. Most people realize that while exams are an imperfect way of making appointments, they are more neutral than the old spoils system.

What is poignant about this case is Officer Brown's insistence on using the test as an appropriate and fair standard for promotion, despite the argument of his colleagues that the exam is "culturally biased" against blacks. My own view of the matter is that Samuel Brown should be promoted, not because of the court-mandated decision, but because in refusing to accept the court's decision, he exemplified the reaction one might wish to see in a police sergeant.

There are times when the police commissioner and the mayor have given citations to police officers for heroic deeds. There are also infrequent occasions when officers have been promoted because of special circumstances. It seems to be that Brown's exemplary behavior is one of those occasions. In defying the admonitions from his colleagues; in refusing to acquiesce to a court order that he believes is wrong, Samuel Brown has displayed the independence of mind that should be a requisite of a senior police official.

Clearly, this example challenges the conventional wisdom. While many black officers have commented that since they're going to be labeled "quota sergeants" anyway, they might as well be given the status and the pay. Self-interest is what usually counts. Samuel Brown, however, has shown that idealism has not yet been interred by cynical quota arrangements.

In a city attempting to adjudicate competing racial and political interests, affirmative action has been the response. There is a widely held view that blacks are the recipient targets because they are unable to compete on their own. Samuel Brown has not put this notion to rest. But in suggesting that blacks should be judged by the same standards as everyone else, he is actually contending that they can and will compete as equals. From my point of view, this is a breath of fresh air. In fact, I wouldn't be adverse to having Samuel Brown as a future commissioner in our police department. He might be just the kind of person this city needs.

February 18, 1987

25

A Justification for Firings

From reading stories about Donald Trump, one could infer he is a miracle worker or the devil incarnate. As is the case with most newspaper characterizations, these are greatly exaggerated. However, from a recent story about Trump's management of the Wollman Ice Skating Rink emerges a picture of the relative efficiency of private enterprise and the relative inefficiency of municipally managed enterprises. If Trump is a miracle worker it is due in no small measure to his latitude as a private broker.

Several weeks ago it was reported that $1,500 was missing from the receipts at the Wollman Rink. After an internal audit, Trump fired his two managers summarily, even though their culpability wasn't clear from the reports. In my opinion this decision symbolizes the advantage private ventures still enjoy. Firing someone or threatening to fire someone for incompetence or suspected incompetence or for failure to meet responsibilities in a public institution is as anachronistic as twenty lashes for not punching in on a time clock.

Union contracts, workers protection, affirmative action, litigation activities—all have conspired to inhibit firing a person for suspected or even real incompetence. That claim doesn't imply that these workplace protections don't have value on an individual basis, but in the aggregate they have undermined efficiency and virtually destroyed the ethos for hard, dutiful work. It is instructive to compare the employee attitude in a city agency—any agency—with that of employees in a private firm. Neither the carrot nor the stick affects the municipal employee.

In most respects the city worker resembles the Soviet apparatchik. His salary is determined by seniority, not performance. For all practical purposes, he can't be fired. And his approach to work is like a sloth on tranquilizers. Since there is nothing to be gained from determined effort, it is rarely found. This public servant serves only one master, himself or herself.

By contrast, Donald Trump possesses the threat of unemployment. He might use it fairly or unfairly; he may even have it used against him by disgruntled employees. But it exists. Admittedly, very few people like to see a person fired for unjust reason. On balance, however, it is probably better from an economic standpoint to retain arbitrary firings than to have public employees with "tenure."

Yet this has been overlooked in New York. Municipal politics have been organized around a self-conscious and much advertised compassion. What New York actually gets for this brand of pseudo-altruistic espousal is gross inefficiency and services more costly than anywhere in the United States. To argue tacitly and overtly that workers cannot be subject to unemployment ensures the influence of municipal unions. In the process it also ensures marginal service and bureaucrats engaged in sleepwalking for pay.

Does this mean that New York would be better run under the leadership of Donald Trump? Not necessarily. It isn't Trump's skills that are in question, but the ability of any mayor to deliver services when incompetence cannot be eliminated. The actual price of this form of "guaranteed job" runs into the many millions of tax-levied dollars. Trump doesn't live with this employment liability. He can demand a lot from his employees because he pays them a lot. He is also free to fire them when it suits his need for business efficiency.

There aren't any miracle workers in New York, although it would be fair to describe someone that way if the person is able to motivate city employees on the present pay scale and with the existing job security. The only axiom that pertains to city employment is that privatizing services will invariably improve efficiency. One reason for this by-now-recognizable condition is that a municipal employee is rarely fired compared to his counterpart in the private sector. If you don't think that matters, try getting a copy of your birth certificate or marriage certificate in New York City's Municipal Building. Here are quintessential examples of protected inefficiency at work.

July 6, 1988

26

Liberals Brook No Criticism of Mr. Cuomo

Alexander Cohen, one of the most prominent producers in Broadway history and the producer for many years of the Tony Awards, resigned from the League of American Theaters and Producers, a trade association. There is nothing particularly exceptional about this occurrence except that this distinguished man, who has been so closely associated with the Tony Awards, will—by this action—be denied a vote in the Tony balloting. Although Cohen refused to discuss the reasons for his resignation, several members of the league attribute it to comments made at the rehearsal for the ceremony.

Cohen's controversial comments begin with an expletive for Frank Rich, theater critic of the *New York Times*, during an off-air segment of the Tony show. He also noted that although Governor Cuomo was to accept an award for the New York State Council on the Arts, he was not in attendance. Cohen was quoted as saying, "The governor of New York hasn't been to the theater in twenty-five years and he didn't want to break his record."

For this Cohen received the opprobrium of League executives, the president of the American Theater Wing, the president and chairman of the Shubert Organization, and almost every other prominent name in the drama business. One can only wonder why this statement should have received such a vigorous response. Moreover, if someone as important to American theater as Cohen cannot speak his mind, who can?

Whether Governor Cuomo goes to the theater or not, whether Frank Rich deserves the obscenity or not, is beside the point. If what theater officials want is blandness, they are well on the way to achieving it. It seems to me that if Alexander Pope were alive both Cuomo and Rich would receive much more biting criticism than Cohen delivered.

Our age is one of demurrals. You can't speak your mind because you may offend a Democrat, a feminist, a homosexual, a prominent person, a journalist, left-handed people, freckle-faced people. While the forces to control censorship are in the ascendancy, self-censorship is on the rise. Clearly it would be distasteful to make ethnic or racial remarks, both beyond the pale. But tastefulness now extends to matters that critics and novelists routinely excoriated in the past. Is it really inappropriate to suggest that the governor wants to keep his record for nonattendance in the theater intact? One of the governor's aides said Cuomo recently saw *My One and Only*. Even if that is true and Cohen's allegation is wrong, it hardly matters.

The danger in the response to Cohen's remarks is that in the supposed interest of responsibility, theater notables are reducing criticism to only what conforms to their present standard of acceptability. Surely an obscenity shouted on-air is offensive and deserves criticism. But Cohen's comment about Frank Rich was said during a break. Should one be held accountable for every comment made during an interlude in the show? If I were to face a penalty for every expletive uttered about an adversary or critic, I would have to spend my remaining days in blocks while academic colleagues throw eggs and tomatoes at my face.

The new censors in our midst have impeccable liberal credentials. They throw benefit performances for the American Civil Liberties Union. If they learn about a campaign to remove a book from a North Dakota library, someone will have a party for the targeted author and state officials will be excoriated amid the chomping on canapés. However, if one were to say our governor is a philistine, that is a statement demanding denunciation. The new censors won't tolerate that kind of backbiting; they make the rules on who should be muzzled.

One would think that with all that Cohen and his wife, Hildy Parks, have contributed to the life of the theater, they would be excused this minor peccadillo. One would also assume that these prominent theater people who often oppose any efforts to limit expression in drama would welcome a Menckenesque remark or two. The problem is that the comments Cohen made were on the index of the new censors. They are unforgiving to the transgressions of their worldview. Alexander Cohen may be one of the important voices in theater, but when he violates the censorship code his colleagues will attack with every ounce of moral zeal they have. Alas, even censorship is an instrument for society elites.

August 1, 1985

27

New York's Socialist Ethos

There are cities in the United States that are enthralled by socialist ideas. Berkeley, California, and Burlington, Vermont, immediately come to mind. But there is only one city of large size that has fallen sway to socialist positions: New York City. While other places are engaged in privatization schemes, New York worships at the shrine of the command economy. Unionists, politicians, government bureaucrats, special-interest groups, poverty hustlers have conspired to dispense favors using the auspices of government.

As a result of this situation there are two kinds of city dwellers: one leading a discounted existence and the other paying through the nose for the privilege of living here. New York's politics can easily be reduced to the lowest common denominator. Those leading a discounted existence wish to protect their privileges and those paying through the nose are doing everything in their power to obtain the discounts. There is no fairness; there isn't civic virtue and there is not an equitable arrangement for managing the system as long as free markets are stifled.

Someone leading a discounted life invariably lives in a rent-controlled apartment. In fact he doesn't even have to live in it, since in many instances, he sublets the apartment for a substantial profit and moves in with his girlfriend. Rent control in New York is equivalent to winning the lottery. If you happen to be born to the right family or pay off the right people, it is a lifetime annuity. On the other hand if you are a poor bloke who moves to New York from Lawrence, Kansas, and you know nothing about the evils of practical socialism, you will pay until your paycheck is squeezed dry indirectly supporting the people who lead a discounted life.

While it was once axiomatic that one applied a week's salary for one month's rent, the newcomers to New York know this proposition is laughable. Most of those who remain unprivileged are slaves of their landlords. I should hastily note that isn't because New York's landlords are greedy, but because the rent-control lobby has forced the market price of unregulated apartments into the stratosphere.

Those with discounts also relentlessly pursue their advantage using every political device at their disposal. One would assume that when a person moved out of a rent-controlled apartment or died, rent control's legal provisions would end. But that isn't the case either. Rent control is passed on to children as a form of twentieth-century primogeniture. One would also assume that with retirement many people would prefer to live in warm climates, places like Arizona and Florida. But these people can't afford to give up their privilege. Who, after all, would reject this financial windfall?

The consequence of these policies is that New York is a mean-spirited place, living proof that socialism promotes envy. Whereas other cities use patronage in the form of jobs to mollify various group interests, New York employs the machinery of government. To make matters worse, New York politicians pretend their actions are highminded. In living memory I can't recall one pol who said that rent control is a financial privilege conferred to one group that gets from another group that gives. Since one out of every seven New Yorkers lives in either a rent-controlled or rent-stabilized apartment, excluding those in public housing, the magnitude of the problem and power of the lobby is evident, despite the fact that the bulk of the population is forced to pay enormous rentals and the supply of new apartments remains hopelessly inadequate.

Few politicians have the courage to tackle the problem, even though many understand it. There is no political capital in offending the rent-control lobby and there is little gain in trying to win the support of newcomers who believe this is the way things are. It's also hard to convince a person who doesn't understand New York that a hidden tax exists on the unprivileged for simply living in this town.

Despite all the claims that New York is a resourceful and imaginative place—claims that are partially true due to the talent pool here—this is in most respects a static community organized along the lines of legal favors. There is very little evidence of community pride that transcends self-interest because socialism demands the adjudication of differences through political muscle, not public spirit. At some point New York will either change its ways or end up like every other socialist failure. It is already clear that if "you can make it here" you can make it in Moscow, Warsaw, Leipzig, or Prague. But the likelihood is these skills aren't transferrable to other American cities.

July 20, 1988

28

The Tyranny of Community Boards

The community boards in New York are an example of giving unrepresentative groups with an antigrowth, antidevelopment bias, power over zoning, land use, social services, and budgetary issues. If one wanted to stifle development in this town there is scarcely a more devious way to do so than through community boards. By any standard these boards exceed the authority outlined for them in the City Charter. In fact, it is their unwritten and informal influence, their lucubrations at public meetings, their hard-headed bargaining ploys, and their negotiating tactics that provide the boards with influence.

That influence is raw, unvarnished political power. Community board meetings attract elected officials, members of the City Council, state assemblymen and senators. In addition the borough presidents have staff members assigned to boards and send their own representatives to the monthly meetings.

Perhaps the clearest example of the arbitrary use of board power is in the disapproval of the twin-towers plan over the New York Coliseum and the reasons given for this decision. The architectural proposal calls for replacing the Coliseum with a building containing office space, a hotel, luxury condominiums, stores, an atrium, and a ten-movie-theater complex. Because the project presumably affects Central Park and mass transit in the general midtown area, the plan was referred to three community boards whose borders intersect near Columbus Circle.

In their final reports board members said "they were opposed to the plan because it would add significantly to traffic congestion and noise and air pollution and would throw shadows on surrounding buildings and Central Park." These are the same predictable claims found in every board report. Traffic on Columbus Circle and the accompanying noise cannot possibly be made worse with a new building. As far as the "shadows" ruse is concerned, it should be pointed out that shadows move because of the disposition of the sun. If the board argument makes any sense, then airplanes shouldn't be permitted over New York because they cast shadows on the city below.

Board members also claim to be concerned about gentrification, the bogey-man that unseats the lower-middle class for the aspiring Yuppies. Yet if gentrification has any effect it is on making the lower-middle-class artisan and homeowner wealthy through the escalation of prices for his services and dwellings. Board members were equally critical of the "paltry" $30 million the developer agreed to spend on the renovation of the subway station. Yet with $30 million the entire Columbus Circle station can be constructed with gold-plated squares.

Members of Board 5 contend that the city and the Metropolitan Transit Authority (MTA) "Have been grossly insensitive to how any redevelopment will relate to its environment in regard to aesthetics, architectural context and potential for significant public amenities." But where do these board members come off making such judgments? Are they trained architects? Is their sense of aesthetics more refined than that of architects working on the project? In anticipation of such concerns raised by the board, Moshe Safdie, a world-renowned architect, was selected for the project. It is virtually impossible for a major developer in this city to use an up-and-coming architect without notable credentials. Should the developer attempt to do so, he would be roasted by the community boards.

City officials have noted that this project could generate hundreds of millions for mass-transit construction and provide $100 million annually in tax revenues. But that doesn't mean anything to board members, who contend that their concerns are glossed over or that profit is the overarching concern. Since these board representatives have arrogated to themselves the voice of the people, any rejection of their unreasonable demands is deemed to be indifference. As one might guess, profit is wrong, since the wealth generated by the construction of such towers adversely affects "the quality of life" of these local residents. Yet unrecognized in this argument are the millions of dollars that will be spent to improve the neighborhood.

The closer one gets to the issues the more apparent it is that something else is at work in these community board deliberations. What is actually happening is the effort of a small but vocal minority who claim to speak for their community, who use their new-found importance to squeeze concessions out of wealthy real estate moguls. The motivation for their actions is sheer green envy. Purporting to use democracy as their defense, they actually use it as a weapon to humble the powerful. Is it therefore at all surprising that developers don't want to work in this city? Is it coincidental that buildings put up in one year two decades ago now take ten years to construct? Is it inaccurate to suggest that a three-month delay on the Coliseum project has already cost the city $33 million in tax revenue? Most important, who elected these board members to represent New Yorkers in the first place?

October 2, 1986

29

Reformers on the March

"Political reform" are words pegged into the lexicon of American life. They are judged to be affirmative, since reformers invariably adopt the mantle of magnanimity, which in the present vernacular takes the form of yet another cliché, the public welfare. Yet it should be apparent to anyone who has observed the efforts of reformers, especially in places like New York City, that the sentiment for change under the guise of public-spiritedness invariably disguises the real motive of self-interest.

In no reform I can think of is this condition more apparent than the New York City Council's public-financing bill. On the face of it, the bill provides public funds to candidates in municipal elections who voluntarily agree to limits on campaign contributions and spending. Reformers who supported this legislation contend this measure will alter the way candidates for city office raise and spend money, diminish the influence of major contributors, force politicians to seek small gifts from many people, and enhance opportunities for newcomers to challenge incumbents.

Yet it is clear that the bill does none of these things; nor can it. The City Council is presently controlled by a 34 to 1 majority of Democrats. The vote on the bill was 24 to 9 with two members absent. By any stretch of the imagination this is partisan legislation serving political ends in a city controlled by one party. The bill itself grew out of the city's corruption scandal in this Democratic administration. It is therefore astonishing that the Democrats are asked to reform practices of which they have been found culpable. This is akin to asking a bank robber what security arrangements should be employed in a new bank. The bill certainly deserves the designation given to it by State Senator Roy Goodman: "an incumbents' protection bill."

Among the law's provisions is one that restricts individual contributions to $3,000 per primary or general election for candidates who want public financing, with a different cap on spending for specific offices. The problem with this provision is that it is difficult for new faces to raise small sums from many contributors in order to qualify for matching public monies. On the other hand, incumbents generally have enough money in their treasuries to qualify for matching funds. This is an example of blatant feeding at the public trough by well-heeled politicians.

The bill also reduces the spending limit for challengers, while permitting incumbents to spend up to $50,000 in the year preceding the election and unlimited amounts during the first two years of their term to enhance the ritualistic acts of self-promotion. Compounding this incumbent's advantage is a provision for matching funds in a primary. Since Democrats have primaries and Republicans generally don't, a Democratic candidate has twice the public funding and twice as large a spending limit as his Republican opponent. So much for fairness in this "two-party system.

Although these provisions are optional, since any candidate can decline public funds, the political environment puts a challenger who rejects matching money in an extremely sensitive position. After all, how can one run as a representative of the people and then take large sums from "fat cats" to whom one owes big favors? Even if that claim is untrue, the allegation will assuredly be made and serve as a campaign issue. I can see it now, a Democratic incumbent will get up on his soapbox with feigned indignation to say, "New York can't be bought." Of course he's right, since the Democrats won't sell.

Although this bill has been called an "antidote to sleaze" by the *New York Times*, it will have the opposite effect. The bill entrenches incumbents. It makes it virtually impossible for a newcomer to enter city politics. It ensures Democratic control of the city; in fact, it ensures monopolistic control of the city. Here are incumbents using the power of their office to inhibit opposition. It is without question a manifest perversion of the democratic spirit.

Yet the reformers are congratulating themselves on promoting the public welfare. They wave the banner of fair play. But in fact they have engaged in an act of dissimulation as egregious as any attributed to Boss Tweed; they have simply ridden their Trojan horse through the barrier of political opposition. The net effect of this decision will be a city depleted of Republican opponents and a government ripe for the pickings of corrupt politicians.

July 8, 1988

30

Who Is Buying Influence in New York?

An investigation of campaign contributors in New York City shows that lawyers are rather parsimonious in their contributions compared to members of the financial services and real estate communities, but despite denials, this money probably buys some influence. What these contributions also demonstrate is the extent to which New York is a one-party town in which those who do business with the city, for themselves or clients, have been consistent contributors to Mayor Edward Koch, City Council President Andrew Stein, and Comptroller Harrison Goldin.

Among the major contributors between January 1983 and January 1988 were partners at Shea & Gould, who gave a total of $35,000; partners at Stein, Davidoff & Malito, who gave $23,300; and Brown & Wood, who gave $22,000. While appearances can simultaneously reveal and becloud the truth, it surely seems suspicious that law firms with many partners will bundle $1,000 contributions each and then receive a large contract with the city.

Is it an act of fair play that the Circle Line has a "temporary" lease for thirty-two years at a rate of $15,000 when bids of $250,000 to $300,000 a year for its privileges have been made? Is the line's representation by "Democratic law firms" a factor in these decisions? How did Buzzy Keefe obtain a forty-five-year lease for the River Café? Was his argument so compelling or did he have the "right" lawyers' help? Why are deputy commissioners in the city administration permitted to have private business dealings with law firms routinely engaged in contracts with the city government?

Naturally, lawyers contest the implications in these questions. Davidoff asked, "Am I buying a vote? I cannot believe any one of these people are [sic] going to vote for an issue because we give money." Perhaps on a given vote Davidoff's view is correct, but on the matter of influence-peddling where a contract award is at stake, his assessment may be disingenuous. For example, Robinson, Silverman, Pearce, Aronsohn, and Berman, a seventy-five-year-old law firm specializing in real estate, contributed $5,000 to Koch on

December 10, 1987, three months before the Board of Estimate approved a $30,000 contract for the firm to represent the Teachers' Retirement Board. In response to such acts, State Senator Roy Goodman proposed a $3,000 cap on individuals and corporations that appear before the board within eighteen months of making their contribution. This may be a step in the right direction, but it is probably too little, too late.

It is noteworthy that the Board of Estimate, on which the mayor, comptroller, and council president each have two votes, has the authority to award city contracts, and to make land-use decisions. However, it is virtually impossible for the uninitiated to sort out the deliberations and decision-making process at the board, since there isn't an accessible system of records for the proceedings. In fact, the most recent index for the *Journal of Proceedings* is for the year 1976. Unless one is there following the events themselves it is very hard to determine what is going on. And even then it can be perplexing.

A city finance law passed in February 1988 gives candidates the option of participating in a matching-funds program provided certain restrictions are observed. A candidate who chooses to receive these funds is limited to $3,000 per contributor. Those Democrats not accepting public funds can receive up to $50,000 from each contributor. However, despite the restrictions, a candidate can bundle $3,000 contributions at a law firm with many partners, without jeopardizing his right to public funding. According to Lawrence Mandelker, the mayor's campaign treasurer, "This whole thing is ridiculous. . . . What's the difference between a law firm giving a check and a partner going home and writing a check for $3000?" The answer is probably "Not much."

But what Mandelker and others are not sensitive to are the issues of corruption, influence-peddling, and conflict-of-interest decisions. Votes might not be bought for $20,000, but campaigns cannot be organized without these contributions, and some law firms that make them are dependent on city contracts for their revenues. At the very least this situation is unwholesome. Without pointing fingers, it would be wise for the municipal government to appoint a board that will examine the relationship between contracts and contributions. The evidence may be circumstantial, but in the world of politics, like the world of entertainment, appearances do count. At the moment the Koch administration and the one-party Democratic monopoly in New York do not look good.

September 3, 1988

31

Maintaining the City's Public Works:
A Story of Neglect

The closing of the Williamsburg Bridge has been a major tragedy for many New Yorkers. Crossing the East River at the moment is more difficult than it was in the nineteenth century, before the construction of the bridges that connect Manhattan with Brooklyn and Queens. But what makes the closing of the Williamsburg Bridge particularly upsetting is that it could have been avoided.

Mayor Koch admitted that there has been twenty years of deferred maintenance on the bridge; clearly a condition for which he is partially culpable. But what the mayor didn't say, in fact what no one to my knowledge has said, is that federal funds were available for bridge repair, but the Koch administration did not apply for them.

Both the 1982 and 1987 Surface Transportation Acts contain funds for bridge maintenance and repair. The funds exist in two categories: formula funds allocated to states on a percentage basis, for which New York receives 10 percent of the money, and discretionary funds available on an emergency basis. In the latter category money is given on a rank-order basis with the cost of bridge repair and daily traffic key factors in the equation.

The Williamsburg Bridge was specifically mentioned in the legislative history that served as a preamble to the 1982 Act. In the language of the act the Williamsburg Bridge was mentioned "as a high priority." Yet to this day discretionary funds have not been received by the New York City government. And, strange as it may seem, the reason funds have not been allocated is that a repair plan hasn't been submitted to the federal authorities.

In the 1987 Act, $1.6 billion was made available for bridge repairs. Of this total $1.375 billion was in formula funds and the remaining $225 million was part of the discretionary program. While New York's bridges in Queens, Manhattan, and Brooklyn are receiving modest maintenance assistance under the provisions of formula funding, New York is not taking advantage of discretionary funds, particularly the money set aside for emergency measures, which obviously apply to the Williamsburg Bridge.

What is even more startling than the present administrative complacency is that city officials have been aware of the Williamsburg Bridge's deterioration for years, as its mention in the 1982 Act can testify. But plans for repair or reconstruction have been bogged down in a futile political debate. A bridge inspection in 1979 showed major structural flaws, and the subsequent report indicated significant renovation was needed. While political responsibility is always divisible by a number larger than one, the Koch administration must assume major responsibility for this problem, which has disrupted the travel patterns of a quarter of a million commuters and has cost the city's businesses millions of dollars.

While reports on the nation's infrastructure abound and the level of consciousness about public works has increased, it is clear that the allocation of funds to rectify the disrepair is in itself insufficient to solve the problem. This issue requires an attentive municipal administration, one that spends the money wisely and seeks federal funding when it's available. The people of this town deserve nothing less.

If the New York administration is not attentive to the aging condition of its public works, this city may cease to be a commercial center. This would not be the first time a city unwilling to invest in its bridges and highways destroyed the infrastructure that was the catalyst for its prosperity in the first place. But such inactivity in New York could be cataclysmic for the nation. The loss of New York as a commercial center holds deep symbolic meaning for all Americans.

Clearly the time for action was yesterday. What is dismaying about the Williamsburg Bridge is not simply its disrepair, but the fact that this city administration has lost sight of public-works maintenance and has neglected to apply for federal funds earmarked for emergency purposes. That the Williamsburg Bridge stands after all these years of continual strain on its foundation from subway and car use honors the memory of those engineers who designed and constructed it. If the bridge is still standing twenty years from now, it will mean the city administration will have finally taken seriously its public trust to ensure the safety and survivability of this town's infrastructure.

June 29, 1988

32

The Politics of Cynicism

The spectacle of Jesse Jackson meeting with Mayor Koch gives new meaning to politics in the 1980s. While politics has always engendered some degree of cynicism, this alleged rapprochement stands as an unprecedented event. On the one side is the mayor of New York, defender of Jewish positions and an unmitigated critic of the Reverend Mr. Jackson and many of his most vocal defenders including Louis Farrakhan, ardent hate-monger. On the other side is Jackson, the self-possessed claimant for the highest office in the land who uses racial designations the way baseball players use bats.

The catalyst for this meeting is Governor Cuomo, the man struggling to be entitled the *eminence gris* in the Democratic party. Presumably Cuomo wants to heal the rift between these men so the party can get on with its real mission, which is winning the presidency for Michael Dukakis. It doesn't hurt Cuomo's chances for the Democratic nomination in 1992 if he can present himself at the peacemaker in New York politics.

These negotiations are being handled with all the protocol of the Versailles Treaty. No one wants to offend and neither side wants to concede. Yet the victor is clear: Jesse Jackson has brought Koch to his knees. If Koch wants to be mayor for an unprecedented fourth term he had to eat crow. Koch ate enough to have indigestion for the next four years. After having said during the New York primary that any Jew voting for Jackson would have to be crazy and after noting that four weeks into a Jackson presidency the country would be defenseless and in six weeks bankrupt, the mayor extends his hand in friendship and calls Jackson a great statesman.

What gives this peace meeting special poignancy is that Koch appeared to be a man who spoke his mind whatever the consequences. His political strength seemed to be in his honesty. As he and his media flaks pointed out many times, Koch is not like other politicians. The Jackson meeting brought that bit of imagery to a shattering conclusion. There is only one reason for Koch to swallow his pride and that is reelection. He doesn't want to confront a black candidate in the primary and perhaps in the general election who is supported by Jackson and his black minions. A David Dinkins or a Charles Rangel probably can't defeat Koch, but either could wound him beyond redemption against a formidable Republican.

Jackson, for his part, revels at the prospect of Koch groveling for his endorsement. His goal is undisguised power. And what better way to secure it than having Koch register black voters who can be used by Jackson in a national election. This is the price Jackson probably secured for having a meeting and "photo opportunity" with Koch. Any way one looks at it, the deal has a strange aroma. Despite all the claims about the new Jackson, the conciliatory Jackson, the statesman, the healer, Jackson has the instincts and has demonstrated the behavior of a Stalinist. His policies and his speeches prove that he is not in the political mainstream, even a mainstream pushed to the left by cultural changes over the last three decades. Moreover, his record of anti-Semitic comments, not only his unwillingness to repudiate Farrakhan, illustrates deep-seated sentiments that should be censured by any sensible person. I would guess that Jews who did support Jackson in the primary were ignorant of his public comments about Jews.

Now New Yorkers are asked to believe that the anti-Semite and the self-appointed defender of the Jewish people have interests in common, interests that transcend "petty" disagreements. Alas, "cynicism" is the only word that does justice to this political event. In my opinion if the only way Koch can win his 1989 election is with Jackson's endorsement, he shouldn't run. No office is worth that kind of humiliation. Would La Guardia have asked for Father Coughlin's support in his effort to win a fourth term? The parallels are not far-fetched. With the Koch-Jackson entente cordiale, Ed Koch is either a liar or an unalloyed opportunist. In either case his vulnerability is being worn like a hirsute.

It's hard to find a pearl in this poisoned oyster. However, there are signs that New Yorkers are sick of Koch and sick of New York's one-party system in which voters' sentiments can be so blatantly manipulated. In a strange way Koch and Jackson deserve each other. What binds them is the desperate, monomaniacal quest for office. Jackson wants it and will use any cheap demogogic trick to get it, and Koch wants to hold on and is not above any act that will allow him to do so. That is why these strange bedfellows met, Cuomo's comments to the contrary notwithstanding. Until Koch is ousted and Jackson is a footnote to history, this recent meeting will stand as quintessential example of the politics of cyncicism.

September 7, 1988

33

Why the Mayor Shouldn't be Given
a Fourth Term

There is no question that Mayor Edward Koch has the courage of his convictions. Despite all the claims of divisiveness, the mayor's comments about Jesse Jackson during the New York primary were accurate. There may be some Democrats who don't like his style, but there are few critics who can challenge his sincerity.

If there is a legitimate concern about the mayor's much discussed ineffectiveness, it probably has little to do with his public comments. The mayor speaks his mind, which in a city accustomed to pandering politicians is bound to lead to controversy. But on one matter the mayor has affirmed the view of his critics: he isn't watching "the store." The mayor so enjoys the limelight, so glories in his ceremonial duties as "hizzoner," that administrative responsibility is neglected.

Very recently the mayor called the city's chief engineer a "dummy" for not realizing the Williamsburg Bridge was seriously corroded. Although he did apologize for this remark, he noted "the chief engineer pointed to deterioration of the cables atop the bridge," but now we find "the corrosion is underneath." Furthermore, Mayor Koch said it was "inexplicable" that his administration should be held responsible for the corrosion, since paint for routine maintenance is available. "We would have given them all the paint they wanted. They never asked for it."

What is inexplicable in this incident is the long-standing neglect of a much discussed problem. Whether paint is available or not, whether the mayor was directed to the cables on top instead of the supports below, are somehow beside the point. The mayor didn't pay attention to this issue; he simply neglected the matter until lives were in jeopardy. Had the mayor fulfilled a promise to examine the structural soundness of New York's bridges, the closing of the Williamsburg Bridge might have been avoided.

While Koch deserves the title of "teflon mayor," the corruption in his administration deserves careful scrutiny. I'm confident the mayor is impeccably honest, but the scandals that have accompanied several of his appointees and City Council members are due in no small part to a mayor who has overlooked his role as administrative monitor. Commissioners do, of course, report to the mayor regularly, but the mayor rarely has the time or inclination to examine the performance of his appointees. It is precisely when people are evaluated for efficiency that corruption and incompetence are found.

Yet another example of this administrative neglect is the Billie Boggs case. While the mayor's instincts, in my opinion, were correct, the entire matter was handled maladroitly. Ms. Boggs should have been picked up off the streets involuntarily. She was a scourge in the neighborhood and she was doing damage to herself, notwithstanding claims to the contrary from New York Civil Liberties lawyers who have their own ax to grind. However, in this case the city's psychiatrists were pitted against the NYCLU attorneys. It was—as one might guess—a standoff.

Had the administration's attorneys obtained testimony from those in the community who were accosted by Boggs, the mayor could have made his case more effectively. Instead divergent "expert" opinions resulted in a stalemate. The judge was left with no alternative, but to release Boggs. Moreover, the evidence on appeal will be restricted to testimony from the first trial, which means in effect that the psychiatrists will engage in another round of inconclusive accusations. In the end the mayor will come away from the case with egg all over his face despite his decent instincts.

It is obvious that it takes more to be mayor of New York than good instincts. A mayor must also be somewhat more than a Falstaffian actor who gravitates to the klieg lights. While many poke fun at management skill—and that in itself is an insufficient condition for political success—New York desperately needs a mayor who can and will manage the affairs of this city.

Mayor Koch deserves credit and thanks for leading New York away from the financial abyss in the 1970s. He has certainly set the right tone for order on the streets with his advocacy of the death penalty. Yet his managerial deficiencies indicate New York would be better served with another mayor. It has often been said, "If it ain't broke, don't fix it." That is a sentiment with which I agree. But much of New York is broke and requires fixing and the way to begin is with another mayor.

May 25, 1988

34

Extra-Democratic Methods for the Selection of New York's Mayor

It was recently reported that the mainstays in the Republican party of New York State and City held a meeting in which they agreed to form a "bipartisan fusion coalition" to defeat Mayor Koch. These GOP leaders—including the five county leaders and the state party chairman, Anthony Colavita—seem to believe that any effort to unseat Koch and avoid a multicandidate free-for-all is desirable.

Although it is difficult for me to discuss this matter as a disinterested party since I am actively seeking Republican party endorsement in the 1989 mayoralty race, I am appalled by this decision of party panjandrums. There are many reasons for this response that have little, if anything, to do with my personal involvement in the matter.

For one thing the problems of New York, a litany of which is known to any city resident, are due in some part to the existence of a one-party monopoly. While corruption can and does exist in multiparty states, it is fostered, indeed encouraged, by a one-party system. The corruption within the Koch administration cannot be explained without some reference to the abysmal state of the Republican organization.

It might also be noted that this decision to support a fusion candidate, who will in all likelihood be a Democrat, is an insult to rank-and-file Republicans who have been working in the trenches for an independent Republican party and a real alternative to ritualistic Democratic voting. That the name of the recently resigned City Charter Revision Commission chairman, Richard Ravitch, is the one that has surfaced in these "secret" deliberations is particularly distressing. Ravitch is a lifelong Democrat who has not shown any interest in the Republican party previously.

This decision by local Republican leaders also flies in the face of efforts to build an organization capable of contesting other city and congressional races.

73

The next mayoralty race was to be a laboratory for urban Republican politics, a testing ground for policies that might affect other urban areas largely dominated by Democratic machines. If the Democratic stranglehold on New York could be broken, or at the very least loosened, the road to a two-party system in metropolitan urban areas might well be paved.

If the Republican leadership is serious about its decision to support a Democratically led fusion ticket in New York City, it will be a significant setback to two-party politics in this town. Moreover, it will also militate against desperately needed alternative policies and short change New York residents.

My hope is that Democrats and Republicans won't take this decision lying down. They should denounce this measure as an antidemocratic act that is masquerading as "a good government" measure. Should General Secretary Gorbachev argue that the Soviet system requires only one party, since that party is the embodiment of the people, we in the West would immediately understand his real intent. But when our party leaders use their influence to transcend democratic procedures, it is accepted as a serious proposal.

It may well be that Richard Ravitch would make a good mayor. On that point the jury is out. But Ravitch should have to work for his party's nomination and have to test his arguments against a rival like any other candidate in a free election. It is absurd to hand any office to a potential candidate, on a silver platter.

I am prepared to enter a primary struggle against any Democrat selected by the Republican leaders. In fact I now call on each and every Republican to repudiate this "fusion" deal. There aren't many registered Republicans in this city and for good reason. Republican leaders have bigger fish to fry than party loyalty.

However, one doesn't need an extensive memory to recall that in 1981 Edward Koch received bipartisan support. There isn't a scintilla of evidence to suggest that Republican endorsement had a salutary effect on the party or, for that matter, did this decision benefit New York City. On the contrary the Manes-related scandal and evidence of widespread city corruption appeared soon after the obvious Koch mandate.

New York doesn't need a fusion candidate to solve its woes; it needs ideas competing in an electoral crucible. It doesn't need a savior on a white horse or white subway car to save the city; it requires a democratic process in which the people speak. This town wasn't organized for party bosses; it is a bastion of opinion—a place where ideas count. To argue as some Republican pundits have that they know what is best for New York is a position that can never stand the light of day and, if good sense prevails, will be interred along with other proposals that violate the sense of fair play in this city.

December 3, 1988

Part III

Urban Economics

35

Instead of Taking Jobs, Immigrants Improve Our Standard of Living

Julian Simon, author of *The Ultimate Resource*, has completed a work dealing with immigration in the United States. He contends that despite some widely embraced views, immigrants generally improve the national standard of living.

Clearly, Simon does not favor welfare abusers or illegal aliens. But his thorough analysis challenges several assumptions that deserve careful scrutiny. He argues that "within three to five years after entry, immigrant family earnings reach and pass those of the average native family. . . ." He also contends that immigrants generally do not take jobs from Americans or push wages down and that they are not uneducated and unskilled. Exactly how beneficial immigrants are to this society and the economy will be debated for some time. But what Simon has done is change the nature of the debate by demonstrating that many of the alleged costs are unfounded and many of the potential benefits underestimated.

This, by the way, squares with my own experience. New York City has become a different and, by and large, better place over the last twenty years as a result of the new immigrants. New York, as the Statue of Liberty attests, has always been a refuge for immigrants. But most people are unaware of the new immigrants who have changed this city. Although there are many illustrations, including the Vietnamese, Hong Kong Chinese, and Cubans, the three groups I am most familiar with may be most revealing.

The first is the Greek immigrants, who came to these shores in large numbers during the repressive military regime in the '60s. Although they infrequently had formal education, they were accustomed to working hard and had experience in their own tavernas. It is precisely this kind of experience that has been translated into all-night eateries in New York that serve tasty food at reasonable prices. Most important, these people are willing to work long and hard. While many chic restaurants close promptly at 10:00 P.M., the Greek diners are open all night for post-theater coffee, truckers who want a sandwich, or late-night daters eager for a snack.

Then there are the Koreans, who have come to dominate the produce stands around the city, serving fresh fruit and vegetables rarely seen in New York before. These people are efficient, energetic, and happen to have superb products. Moreover, these establishments are family operations with Mom, Dad, and children involved. When the children are of college age, they are obliged to go to a university. By the way, almost 90 percent of the eligible Korean population attends college.

The City University of New York, which was in the doldrums after "open admissions" was introduced twenty years ago, has been going through a resurgence because of the Korean student population. As one Brooklyn College professor told me, "These people have given intellectual vitality to our school that I thought was buried in the early seventies."

Soviet Jews represent the last of my illustrations. These people moved into Brighton Beach, a community in Brooklyn on the seashore. For years Brighton suffered from urban blight. Former residents—and I am one—referred to it as "Blighton Beach."

With the Soviet migration allowed after the Jackson-Vanak Amendment, Brighton has become Odessa on the Atlantic. Russian is the language one hears most on the boardwalk. The streets are clean for the first time in fifteen years. Clubs serving vodka, pirogen, derma can be found along the central avenue. Last weekend I attended one of these clubs and found myself transported to a Russian Xanadu where dance, good food, and fine music could be found in abundance. Released from hell, these Soviets use their new-found freedom to create a world they once dreamed about.

Why should it be any other way? This land is unique. Its freedom offers what cannot be found anywhere else on this globe. There are detractors in our midst who do not appreciate immigrants and do not value what is distinctive about this nation. They often argue this is no longer a land of opportunity. For these people I say, take a walk on Brighton Beach Avenue, eat kiwi from a Korean fruit stand, or taste some baklava from a Greek diner. Then tell me there is no opportunity or that immigrants cannot "make it" in this nation.

July 12, 1984

36

"Full Employment" in New York City

For several decades economists have been arguing that "full employment" is equivalent to an unemployment rate of 4 percent. There is nothing magical about that number, but it seems that with structural, seasonal, and entrenched unemployment it is virtually impossible to achieve rates below that level. It is therefore rather astonishing that the recently announced unemployment rate for New York City is 3.5 percent.

What this means, in effect, is that in New York jobs are increasing at a rate faster than the number of people entering the job market and that the need for workers may exceed the qualifications of those seeking employment. There is little doubt that this condition—should it represent a trend—has significant implications. Perhaps the most significant conclusion is that the liberal edifice for social reform has been blown to bits.

For decades liberals have entertained visions of an activist government providing succor to the poor who were unable to find employment. Relying on an economic determinist's view, crime is a function of poor people asserting themselves against the vicissitudes of an unjust and volatile market system. Hunger is a function of people unable to secure a job. Educational failure is related to students who presumably have no hope for future employment.

So widespread is this mythology that New York's welfare apparatus continues to grow despite an economic backdrop in which jobs are mushrooming. It is instructive that "Help Wanted" signs have become a permanent part of the decor in the retail stores of every borough. While unskilled and low-skill jobs are expanding at a slower rate than the much advertised high-tech jobs, they are expanding from a higher base and will therefore grow more in absolute numbers for the rest of this century than jobs requiring advanced education.

New York is the land of opportunity for those who want to work. Entering and staying in the job market at any position is the surest guarantee against poverty. Why then are even 3 percent of New York's residents unemployed and why do so many people stay out of jobs, thereby effectively removing themselves from the ranks of the unemployed? It is increasingly clear that government programs designed to help the poor have encouraged the very values and social characteristics that militate against employment. The political *Weltanschauung* in New York for much of the last three decades is one of victimization in which poor persons are not responsible for their fate. Presumably racism, inequality, market fluctuations, and bad luck account for poverty; rarely, if ever, is it the fault of those who are poor.

As a consequence of this attitude, a welfare bureaucracy was installed and ensconced in New York that is largely superfluous. The private sector is generating jobs at a rate that exceeds the grandest expectation of most experts. Yet welfare in New York is a sacred cow. Neither the bureaucracy that administers it nor the activists who derive political capital from it can challenge the assumptions on which welfare is based. But it is now admitted by many in the welfare whirlpool that the system promotes passivity and a sense of worthlessness. As Charles Murray, author of *Losing Ground*, showed, welfare has entrenched a permanent underclass in the country, particularly in places like New York City where the benefits have been most generous and where becoming pregnant without a husband results in income and status that would not otherwise be available.

The evils of welfarism have finally crept into the public consciousness, notwithstanding "humanitarian speeches" calling for additional government social spending. But the combination of this recognition along with a "full-employment" rate have shaken the foundations of the liberal belief system. It can no longer be asserted in New York that welfare is necessary to assist those who want to work and cannot find a job. There are jobs for everyone wishing to work.

The problem is that the liberal belief of most New Yorkers nurtured on an activist government has not kept pace with the economic reality. It is incumbent on municipal leaders to advertise the "full-employment" status in this city and to argue that further largess for the poor doesn't do them any good and isn't related to New York's present economic condition. Of course, that is what should be argued if politics could be set aside. But on this matter, like so many others, political aims, not economic reality, determine the City Hall agenda.

August 24, 1988

37

Plenty of Jobs for Teenagers

One of the most widespread economic myths is that there are relatively few jobs available for the exceedingly large number of unemployed youths, particularly minority youths. At every conference on urban problems this argument is made. "We need jobs" is a refrain heard from the corridors of the school auditorium to the union meeting hall. One also hears its corollary: "We don't want dead-end positions; we need real jobs."

Both of these contentions are pure and simple bombast. After a recent investigation I discovered the following evidence: fast-food jobs for teenagers have been increasing. In fact, most chain-store managers complain that there aren't enough kids applying for the jobs that are available. And these are not dead-end jobs.

At Burger King wages start at $3.40 an hour. After three months, an employee is eligible for a raise that can vary based on the manager's evaluation.

After one year, a good employee is eligible to be an assistant manager with an average salary of $13,000 a year. Because of the rapid turnover there is a distinct possibility that one can become a manager in less than two years, earning between $19,000 and $20,000 a year.

At McDonald's the starting wage is also $3.40. After thirty days employees are eligible for an increase of 10 cents, 15 cents, or 25 cents an hour.

A promotion to assistant manager can occur at any time if the employee "demonstrates knowledge of the store and its practices and performs well."

Assistant managers earn an average of $14,000. The elevation to general manager varies, albeit most employees reach that grade before three years and earn between $20,000 and $21,000 a year.

There are similar opportunities at David's Cookies and other firms. These positions, I should hastily point out, are sometimes referred to as "unskilled jobs," which do not require a high school diploma. Why, then, do these jobs go unfilled? There are numerous reasons. One is that many of the unemployed youths do not want to work or do not want to work hard. These jobs are demanding. It is also true that approximately 30 percent of all food-chain robberies are inside jobs. This suggests that it is easier to steal than to work for your money. Some kids do not want to earn money the old-fashioned way.

Another problem is that the incentive to work often doesn't compare with the incentive to engage in illicit activity, primarily selling drugs on the streets. A heroin dealer on the streets of New York can earn $1,000 a day tax-free and determine his own work hours.

Thus finding the adolescent to match the job isn't easy. While a diploma isn't a requisite for employment, hard and dutiful work along with courteous behavior are. It doesn't take much to get ahead at these positions and earn a decent wage. But what I consider "not much" is a great deal to many youths untutored in the ways of appropriate job behavior.

The incompatibility of jobs and youths is a function of upbringing. If courtesy and manners haven't been instilled, even the appearance of respect will be absent. If parents live off the dole or use their wits to survive on the street, working long and hard on a regular job comes to be seen as "chump change" for suckers. If authority of any kind is the enemy, orders from a superior are intolerable.

These are the real issues on the job market, the issues that civic leaders will not address. There are jobs, many of them. If this does not square with your experience ask about employment at Haagen Dazs, David's Cookies, Burger King, Wendy's—the list goes on.

The import of my survey is startling. The youth unemployment problem is largely fictional. If kids are ready to work, there is work for them. And if they work hard, there are financial rewards available to them.

It may make some people feel righteous to complain about youth employment. They ought to have a closer look at reality.

October 4, 1987

38

Put Cork on the Bottle Law

Making public policy is like applying pressure to playdough. A force in one direction has consequences in another.

Last year, New York adopted the return-can-and-bottle formula already employed in several states. The deposit on each container was to contribute to the cost of cleaning up unsightly debris.

It was expected that with each can worth a nickel, people wouldn't throw them away, and even if they did, others would collect them and get the deposit.

In principle this measure has all the elements of the free market that I usually embrace. However, in this case a measure designed to make New York cleaner has had the opposite effect.

Those who collect cans search for them everywhere. No stone is unturned, no garbage can is left unopened, no plastic bag closed.

A neat stack of plastic bags on the curb is now a possible treasure trove of cans and bottles. The debris that flies through the air is of little concern to these street explorers. Garbage is no longer in one place: it is ubiquitous. It was once said: bag it and forget it. Alas, that is simply no longer true. The bag is a target of profit.

What this means, of course, is that garbage is entropic. It is part of the air we breathe. Occasionally some clever engineer will discuss using garbage to create or to build a ski slope in Central Park. But those proposals are related to garbage that has been collected. The garbage to which I refer is random, picked-over garbage that swirls in the wind. Garbage has an effect on our city's income. The more of it you have on the streets the fewer tourists you have in your hotels. It should be possible to obtain support for measures that reduce random garbage on the streets if doing so also benefits the city's economy.

The group most adversely affected by this formulation is the growing army of vagrants that live off these beverage-container deposits.

Certainly something must be done about these people who are, generally speaking, the result of other social policies such as ''deinstitutionalization''— the legal steps taken to free the insane from hospitals in the name of civil liberty.

The combination of these street people with the incentive for easy money to be picked up at will has resulted in our streets becoming open sewers. Unless something is done soon, every street in Manhattan will resemble a garbage dump.

Since I was an early advocate of this plan, it is with great regret that I recommend rescinding the nickel deposit. The net effect would be salutary, even if the occasional soda can or beer bottle is found on a building ledge. It's time for rethinking.

October 31, 1985

39

The Homeless Workers of New York

It is often said that the so-called homeless of New York represent the down-and-out, those who are unemployed and probably unemployable. For many in this category—particularly those who are mentally incompetent—this attribution is probably accurate. But if you've watched the street people of this city, it is obvious that many work and some work very hard.

There are basically three kinds of activity in which they are engaged.

Many street people are in search of beer and soda cans for which there is a nickel deposit. They walk in the streets close to the curb pulling shopping carts filled with cans. From the sun's rising till the darkness of night these people are in a perennial search for cans. They stop at every corner basket, open every plastic garbage bag, rummage through trash cans in the hope a nickel can will be discovered.

The second activity involves paper collection. Here again, pennies are attached to each pound of paper. But this is a relatively easy discovery. Almost everyone throws a newspaper away. The difficult part results from carts filled with paper that require great strength to pull, which means they usually move at a glacial pace. This work is only for youthful vagrants.

An activity shared by the youthful and aged is cleaning car windshields. From Delancey to Houston streets on Third Avenue, a driver is accosted at each corner by these cleaners. I sometimes refer to these stops as New York's toll booths. The rags used by these vagrants are so dirty, it is something of a contradiction to call these people cleaners. Nonetheless, most drivers allow their windows to be soiled. In fact they rarely have a chance to say No. Before you can wave the descending "cleaner" away, a spray has made it impossible to see out the window. Needless to say this can be relatively profitable work. It is customary to give a windshield wiper a quarter. I know this from sad experience. On one occasion when I gave a fellow a dime he threw it away shouting an obscenity at me. Even vagrants have a minimum wage.

While the youthful street people can drive their older counterparts out of these activities through theft and strong-arm tactics, these work practices continue to flourish in many parts of the city, suggesting that where there is income, workers may be found. However, there is a rub.

Many vagrants collect welfare payments in addition to what they can collect from street activity. They are free to work when they want without the constraints of regular hours. In part this explains why there are so many "can hunters" on the street while so many dishwashing jobs go unfilled.

But there is another point in this description. If income, however modest, can generate work, why can't a market for garbage result in a clean city? By treating garbage like soda cans, vagrants could receive payment for depositing debris in designated locations. The question that emerges from this suggestion is "Who pays?" As I see it there are three sources for the money.

The New York City Tourist Board should provide some funding if clean streets can result in increased tourism. In fact, since tourism is one of New York's major industries, it is worthwhile estimating the loss in revenue that results from the despicable condition of the streets. Additional funding should come from the Sanitation Department budget. After all, there will be less for carters to do under such a scheme. Last, the Chamber of Commerce could foot part of the bill, arguing that there is a justification for why "I love New York."

Since there are an estimated 100,000 "homeless" people in New York, many of whom work on the streets day and night, why not give them a chance to earn money from yet another socially desirable activity? This doesn't involve government handouts, nor is another city commissioner needed for this enterprise. All that is required are money, a deposit station, and a way to pay the street carters.

Unfortunately, in a city where social-work sentiments prevail, this activity will be seen by some as demeaning. Sanitation union bosses will fear the competition. City officials will contend this is a lure for vagrants from other areas. In the end the proposal will be discarded. Yet each and every day before the crack of dawn I hear the street scavengers working feverishly in search of empty cans. They work long hours for little compensation and they don't seem to care. Why not give these people another chance to earn some money and in the process give New York a chance to clean its face?

August 11, 1987

40

The Disappearing Newsstands of New York

For the small-time businessman eager to make a buck in New York, the city administration represents the intrusive and strangulating arm of arbitrary authority. Nowhere is this more evident than in regulations for newsstand vendors. A set of proposed rules by the Koch administration is so onerous as to be described as a "war on newsstands." Robert Bockman, counsel to the operators, complains that consumer-affairs officials have unleashed an unprecedented enforcement sweep of street newsstands. In a two-week period the agency uncovered "500 violations and revoked three operators licenses."

If one were to consider the decline in newsstands over the last four decades, it is not exactly an exaggeration to describe the newsstand business as a battleground. In 1950 there were 1,325 sidewalk stands; today there are between 278 and 353, depending on who is doing the counting. In addition to the decline in street stands, subway newsstands have decreased by 45 since 1987. If the proposed regulations are put into effect, newsstands won't be a declining industry, they will be a disappearing industry.

On the face of it the proposal has absurd characteristics. It would include the overhang in estimating the square-footage limit. Newsstands would have to be located fifteen feet from the corner instead of the present five-foot requirement. There is a provision for greater distance between the stand and parking meters than now exists in the regulations. The clearance between stand and building entrances will be lengthened significantly. And the proposed fee for the privilege of doing business would increase from $50 to $925, a 1,700 percent jump.

While some newsstands in prime locations turn a comfortable profit, most street stands provide neither easy money nor easy work. Operators work long hours and are easy targets for thieves. The average newsstand operator nets between $30,000 and $40,000 annually after expenses and works between twelve and fourteen hours a day, very often involving his whole family in the enterprise.

Getting a newsstand license is like trying to get an export permit in the Third World. It usually takes between several weeks and several years, depending on the site and the number of applicants. A proposed site must be reviewed by the Bureau of Highways to ensure the installation doesn't impede traffic. Then the Arts Commission must approve the stand's design. And finally the Department of Consumer Affairs authorizes the construction of the stand, monitors the work, and makes a final inspection before issuing a license.

Historically, newsstands have been a gateway to business activity for recent immigrants. Before 1914 stands were distributed to orphanages. Today the city administration gives priority to disabled veterans, disabled people, veterans, and people over sixty-two. There are more than 400 people on the waiting list for a stand, many of them Indians and Pakistanis who have joined their countrymen in this newspaper-sale enterprise. Yet astonishingly, the city administration is making it more difficult rather than less difficult for these stands to exist.

The fallout of newsstand elimination can easily be calculated, not only on those who will lose an employment opportunity, but on the few newspapers that survive in this city. Without easy distribution channels, newspapers will suffer, as will the advertisers in those papers. But the impulse to appease community boards and merchants complaining about street obstructions is irresistible and at the moment a more powerful voice than newsstand operators. In New York you've got to be loud to get attention.

The blind man in the same stand for thirty-five years or the Pakistani immigrant trying to support his family of five from the revenues at his stand does not constitute a constituency of great political influence. Moreover, regulation is the business of city government. New York is regulation crazy. Instead of adjudicating competing interests, the city administration exacerbates tension by controlling every aspect of entrepreneurial life. Even street musicians are assigned spaces by a city commissioner. There is virtually no aspect of city life that is unregulated except for crime.

This condition leaves newsstand operators without much of a leg to stand on. If new regulations are enforced, the newsstand will soon be a New York memory like the *Herald Tribune*, the charlotte russe, the Brooklyn Dodgers, double-decker buses, the nickel fare, and other aspects of city life that once made New York one of the urban wonders of the world. Leave New York to the regulators and this city will resemble a Third World village more than the portal to the land of opportunity.

September 1, 1988

41

Developers Are Not Devils

One would assume that if you asked the typical New Yorker about the real estate industry in this city he would say: "Kill da bums." So inured are we to the expression of dissatisfaction that any other response seems astonishing. Recently, however, pollster Doug Schoen of Penn & Schoen asked 1,000 randomly selected New Yorkers their impressions of real estate developers.

The respondents were drawn from all five boroughs, representing different racial and ethnic groups. An overwhelming majority rent apartments or homes. A plurality has an annual income between $20,000 and $50,000 and the majority of the respondents are Democrats.

The poll was commissioned by the Real Estate Board but, even allowing for that, the results depart surprisingly from my expectations or the stereotype of public attitudes toward real estate developers. An extraordinary 71 percent maintain that tax incentives are necessary to encourage new housing construction. Between 59 and 62 percent believe tax breaks and energy credits should be offered to commercial tenants to locate in underutilized sites. Seventy percent of the respondents contend that real estate development is vital for the city's economic health. Fifty-seven percent maintain that new construction has made New York a more attractive city. And 46 percent, a large plurality, argue that developers have improved "the quality of life" in the city.

Could it be that despite the tarnished image of developers, the public has a secret admiration for these giants of construction?

This survey seems to indicate that the spirit of enterprise still invigorates the average New Yorker as it does the major developers. Yet if one relies on nighttime soap operas, the perception of these businessmen would be one of unalloyed avarice and greed, hardly the kind of attitudes one would reward with tax incentives.

That New Yorkers are bullish on development demonstrates a great deal about the common sense of citizens in this town. Intuitively New Yorkers realize that government is not going to change this city—if New York improves it will happen because of private enterprise. It may surprise new producers and soap-opera writers, but the spirit of free enterprise is alive and well and residing in the breasts of average people.

The notion that the big real estate men are somehow the culprits in this city, that they own the politicians and control the course of events, is a view one often hears in the news, but it is apparently resisted by average citizens. What makes this condition especially surprising is the fact that the supposed victims of developers' greed are these average people "helpless to escape the limited housing options imposed by realtors." But the average people queried in this poll obviously don't see themselves as victims.

Clearly, stereotypes die hard. The unscrupulous landlord dressed in black who assumes control of the mortgage and residence of a poor, decent, hard-working couple down on their luck is the stuff of plays, novels, and television programs. That average people have resisted this emotional appeal is a tribute to their native intelligence.

If this recent poll is any guide, the average New Yorker has a better grasp of economic conditions in this city than the elites who continually excoriate developers for "outrageous" rentals and condo prices. The world of real estate is supposed to be capitalism at work. When the government interferes through rent-stabilization plans or zoning laws, the incentives to build are often inhibited.

Average New Yorkers, asked how they might assist this industry, answered in the way any person in a free-enterprise system might: Provide financial incentives for the developers. That answer offers reams of information about New Yorkers and their approbation of capitalist enterprise.

February 27, 1986

42

So That's What It's Like to Be a Landlord

The landlord has been and to some degree remains the heavy in literature. He is often characterized as venal, inhumane, greedy, and without morally redeeming qualities.

Every once in a while there is a news story that reinforces this stereotype. What we observe is a landlord who doesn't heat his buildings on the coldest days of winter to save money for his already corpulent investments.

It is easy to dislike this kind of character. What is generally not addressed is whether his stereotype is accurate, and, more important, whether this rentier class even exists. So widespread is the co-op phenomenon that the landlord who rents and maintains his apartment is an endangered species. The co-op council has replaced the landlord in neighborhoods, revealing for the first time that it is not easy or inexpensive to maintain a building in this city. The signs of obvious neglect in many co-op buildings can be attributed to tenant-owners who are unwilling to bear the expense of continual maintenance. This condition now stands in stark contrast to the landlord days when the expense was borne by the "venal" owners, even though rent-control laws prevented these people from passing along the costs to tenants in the form of higher rents.

Now there are interminable meetings in which the co-op council must decide whether to remove the external masonry or whether rewiring the building is cost effective. Building democracy is a substitute for good mainte-nance. It is also apparent that the New York landlord was much less likely to be as wealthy as Donald Trump and much more likely to be one of us. To the astonishment of those nourished on the landlord stereotype, it is a revelation to learn that this figure of universal scorn was really a member of the middle class.

Now that he is almost extinct, his social utility is in full view. The landlord was by and large a small investor who tried to make a buck by having his building appreciate in value. He had a stake in maintaining his property. If it deteriorated, his modest investment melted away. Yet he was systematically harassed by the courts, the media, scholars, politicans. He was considered the scourge of society, a blood-sucking parasite who did not contribute to the creation of wealth and the health of the social polity.

Our judges armed with literary suppositions have generally contended that the tenant is right and the landlord is wrong. Our scholars armed with Marxist and Ricardoian assumptions have viewed the landlords as superfluous to a vigorous economy. Our television producers invariably conceive of landlords as avaricious businessmen insensitive to human beings. Yet whom can we blame for the state of New York housing when the landlord in traditional guise is almost extinct? Is the co-op council easily limned as the target of venality?

Recently a friend of mine who serves on a co-op council said, "What we need is a landlord." What he meant by this is a person who makes decisions and maintains the building with a degree of efficiency rarely encountered in today's co-op.

It is lamentable that with the disappearance of the landlord his contributions are finally appreciated. I don't think this sense of appreciation will influence television producers or judges or even the average person. But those people who care about this city should recall a time when buildings were run effectively, when you didn't meet all night to discuss the color of paint in the hallways, and when one person had a stake in protecting and nurturing his investment in a building.

Surely rent control was the final nail in the coffin of the landlord class. But there were other factors at work. Landlords didn't know how to neutralize the criticism leveled at them. They were acting out of the same profit motive as other businessmen, yet were perceived as different.

It may take a while before their economic role is reevaluated but I am confident that will happen. When that does occur the disappearance of the landlord will be seen as related to the escalating price of housing stock and the decline of New York buildings.

November 1, 1986

43

The Housing Mess in New York

Although almost no one in New York knows for sure, it is reasonable to assume that the city owns more than 100,000 buildings, many of them unoccupied. Now you may ask why the city administration should be in the real estate business. In fact, I'd be surprised if you didn't ask.

There are ostensibly two reasons: the relative cost of maintenance compared to the revenue derived from rent and rent control. Many landlords have had enough; they would rather walk away from a bad investment than be vilified for not providing adequate services. The city housing administration therefore becomes the landlord of the "last resort"—or so it appears—providing discounted rentals for poor people and using tax-levied funds for the maintenance of generally unsafe and unsavory environments.

As one might guess, the city isn't a very efficient landlord. At many of its apartments crack dealers have set up headquarters. Even when city administrators offered newly renovated apartments to homeless people at low or no rental arrangements, these street people refused to accept the offer because of the fear of crack dealers. Robert Moncrief, the deputy housing commissioner, said, "We fix apartments but then we can't get anyone to rent them."

On the other end of the economic scale is the spiraling cost of buying or renting an apartment in New York. It is no longer atypical for a family of four to live in a cramped two-bedroom apartment and pay $3,000 a month for the privilege of living in Queens. Manhattan rental rates stagger the imagination, if one can even find a rental apartment. Of course, skyrocketing real estate prices don't mean very much if you happen to reside in one of New York's 218,000 rent-controlled apartments or 943,000 rent-stabilized units. These people are the urban blessed who have an entitlement for life. That many of these people are among New York's richest and best known should hardly be surprising.

In this city too many people have a vested interest in the lopsided distribution of benefits. "Let someone else pay for it" is a constant refrain. That explains why the status quo is immovable. Well, I am one New Yorker who refuses to accept the present housing condition as unchangeable. The way to change things is to convince the millions of residents in this city who do not have rent-controlled apartments that they are being ripped off by those who do. Obviously the marginal cost of a new apartment is related directly to the stabilized rent on an existing apartment.

There are two strategies the city administration should apply to remedy this problem, albeit I'm not confident it will. It should privatize all city-owned buildings through auction. If the poor people who live in these places at the moment wish to remain, sell the apartments for $1 each with priority given to the present residents. On the other side of the scale, eliminate rent control through "vacancy decontrol." When the resident of a rent-controlled or -stabilized apartment moves or dies, rent control leaves or is buried.

Undoubtedly, some people will be hurt or seemingly hurt by these actions in the short run. But over the long term everyone will benefit. New apartments are likely to be constructed in an atmosphere where markets are allowed to work. Over time rents will undoubtedly diminish. Privilege will be democratized: presumably many of those people with rent-controlled apartments in New York and homes in Connecticut will have to decide which one they want.

Markets are always more fair than governments and invariably more efficient. The problem, of course, is that markets don't vote. A rent-control lobby in New York is a powerful political tool that can intimidate the mayor and potential candidates. Since the non-rent-control tenants don't represent a lobby—although they should—they can't possibly neutralize the rent controllers. That is the nub of the problem.

It is not unusual for New Yorkers to line up for a new edition of the *Village Voice* in order to find a relatively inexpensive apartment to rent. It is not at all unusual for fights to break out over who had first dibs on a sublet. New Yorkers are now slaves to their apartments, obsessed with where they dwell. For everyone in this city knows that an apartment is everything. To be dislodged for whatever reason is to be thrown over the brink into an abyss of terror and unremitting uncertainty. Is this any way to live?

It may not be satisfactory for one's psyche. But New Yorkers are not yet at the point where the rebellion is open. Then again those noises I hear from the rooftop may not be from repairmen at work, but tenants who simply can't take it any more. That may turn out to be a hopeful sign for the future of New York.

May 10, 1988

44

The Endangered Bookstores of New York

Jacques Maritain once said that what distinguishes New York from the other great cities of the world is that it is in constant flux. New York does not treasure its past as is the case in Paris; it treasures the future. There is much in the recent history of this city that supports that claim.

Nevertheless, there are New Yorkers who continually lament the loss of the past. One of the most vocal groups is comprised of bookstore owners and shoppers on Bookstore Row (the area on Fourth Avenue between Ninth and Fourteenth streets). According to these people the used-book store is gone forever, a casualty of bottom-line economics. Presumably good bookstores are as irreplaceable as good books. The culprit in this scenario is rising rentals and, as one might guess, the proffered solutions are government subsidies, the use of government-owned space, and rent control.

However, the analysis of the problem as well as the much discussed answers leave much to be desired. The actual decline in used books did indeed occur for economic reasons. But these reasons are related to the value or lack thereof in used books, as opposed to the obvious rise in rent. The fact is paperback books and discounted hardbacks have virtually eliminated a general interest in used books. It's hard to be in the business of selling a commodity that has limited or nonexistent value.

Yet antiquarian bookselling manages to survive and in some places thrive. The Gotham Book Mart, the Strand Book Store, the Pageant Book and Print Shop, and the Academy Book Store are examples of stores that are prospering. Fred Bass, the owner of the Strand Book Store, the nation's largest used-book store, said, "My rent tripled . . . but I think it's a healthy business." The reason why these stores prosper is that they provide a service to their clients that cannot be offered in the bookstore chain outlets. As one salesman at the Strand said to me, "If you can't find it here, it can't be found."

As is often the case when economic conditions change, businessmen adapt. Many of those stores that were fixtures on Fourth Avenue have been converted into mail-order and catalogue-sales outfits serving an established clientele. Several of the used-book dealers have convertible foldaway street stands that can be taken to the parks or a book fair. Surely the glory days of row after row of used-book stores below Union Square is gone or going. But it would be an error to conclude that used-book sellers are out of business.

The idea of providing rent subsidy or rent control—much the same thing— to bookstore owners in an area being gentrified doesn't make any sense. With Union Square Park now sanitized for law-abiding citizens, the space around Fourteenth Street has escalated in value. It is not coincidental that book-stores would be replaced by high-ticket shops and restaurants. Park Avenue from Seventeenth to Twenty-Third streets is New York's latest restaurant row rapidly replacing Columbus Avenue. This is not a lamentable development; it is part and parcel of a dynamic urban environment.

Efforts to stop or curtail economic trends are doomed to failure as are virtually all efforts to impose the will of a command economy on markets. The tale of used bookstores in New York is in a sense the story of this city. What is fashionable changes. What is affordable changes as well. The low-rent district of today may be the high-rent district of tomorrow. Were it not this way, New York would be a static town.

Undoubtedly interest groups like bookstore owners, community boards, and the rent-control lobby would like to see a city in which their concerns are protected through government intervention. To an extraordinary degree these groups have flexed their political muscle and found responsive city politi-cians. But that is no way to run a city, especially a city as dynamic as this one. Markets may not be the perfect adjudicator of competing interests, but they are far more efficient over the long term than the "invisible foot" of govern-ment interference. The disappearance of Bookstore Row and the survival of used-book stores would seem to prove this point.

May 18, 1988

45

42nd Street Renovation May Be Only Way to Save Times Square

George Will argues that the proposed renovation of 42nd Street is a gross misallocation of public funds. Moreover, he contends that the money—like most government expenditures—won't be used wisely. He has a point. But when you consider events and circumstances in New York City, it is a very insubstantial point indeed.

For 42nd Street is presently similar to Dante's inferno. It is a magnet for criminals in the city. In the days before the Miranda ruling and the prevailing hegemony of civil libertarians over the criminal-justice system, it was possible to boot the bums out. Cops used billy clubs to force vagrants off the streets. When I was a young man 42nd Street was a mecca for interesting films no longer viewable in first-run theaters. One didn't worry about personal safety in those days.

What has happened, of course, is that anarchy prevails on today's streets. Police are hamstrung. Undoubtedly it would be far more sensible to clean up the streets than to reconstruct them. In two hours an unleashed police force could do the trick. But that will not happen and everyone from Will to the riffraff on the streets knows it. Therefore, there is no real alternative to renovation.

Mayor Koch is suggesting that what happened on Columbus Avenue without planning could happen on 42nd Street with planning. There is no way of knowing whether he is right. Yet there is no question that the plan represents a risk worth taking. Anyone who cares about our cities knows that crime is an urban scourge that must be controlled. Apparently the only way to do that is through urban renewal.

In one sense conservatives, who value tradition and lament the displacement of long-time city residents, have a legitimate reason for opposing this kind of project. But what they overlook is that relocation through renovation is the only way now available for dealing with the crime problem. Admittedly, there should be less expensive and elaborate ways to cope with the matter. But there aren't at this moment.

The future of the city depends on its tourist industry, the leading producer of wealth in this American Athens. But to attract people to the city, something must be done about the vagrants, indigents, and hardened criminals who own the streets around Times Square. Any cop in the area will tell you at the slightest prompting that one's safety cannot be assured after 10:00 P.M.

New buildings won't guarantee public safety. But they will force the thugs off the streets—at least temporarily. Moreover, with the streets well lit, drug deals won't be so easy to negotiate. Clean, new buildings might attract the kind of people who once considered 42nd Street a desirable place to visit.

The changes don't perforce mean that civility will return to midtown miraculously. Criminals won't be locked up because of new buildings. And tourists will still be a target for thugs. For the first time since the 1950s, however, there is some hope for Times Square.

The conflict between ideology and pragmatism can lead to bitter disputes. New Yorkers know that all the philosophy in the world won't remedy the problem on their streets, and it is no coincidence that Will is from Chicago. On any level Chicago is not New York.

It would be consistent with common sense to round up the thugs to make the streets safe for the rest of us. But common sense doesn't reign in the post-Earl Warren era.

Seemingly the courts exist to protect the rights of criminals. The only way civic-minded residents can protect themselves is to rebuild the city. It's a sad comment on the times, but it may be the only way to save Times Square.

May 8, 1984

46

The Free-License Zone of New York

In the hands of a resourceful administration New York could be the undefeated champion of free enterprise and a city with a future beyond all reasonable expectations of economic growth. The key to this scenario is a city administration willing to forgo most licensing authority and one that simultaneously serves as a catalyst for enterprise. This, of course, is easier said than done. The history of the last half century in New York indicates a fascination with socialist themes.

However, I have a simple proposal for New York to rediscover the road to free enterprise through a zone—a municipality within a municipality—that permits the sale and licensing of some manufactured products not permitted by federal regulators. Within this zone AIDS patients can purchase drugs that have not yet been approved by the Food and Drug Administration; chemicals banned by the Environmental Protection Agency; toys restricted by the Federal Trade Commission; vehicles that have not met standards established by the Department of Energy. In fact, products that have been banned, restricted, or regulated out of regular channels might be purchased in New York's "free-license zone."

Admittedly, there are risks that accompany such an enterprise, but far fewer than would appear on first glance. The city would not assume any responsibility for product harm. Every product sold would have the following warning attached: "This product has been banned by the Federal Government. You buy it at your own risk. New York offers you the opportunity to buy this product, but makes no claims about its value and will not assume any liability for harm resulting from its use."

This proposal goes beyond a free-enterprise zone that limits or removes the burden of taxes; "the free-license zone" allows people to purchase many items that are banned. The question emerging from this idea is the harm that may occur to unsuspecting purchasers. Since this zone purports to sell that which is banned, the buyer must be wary or foolish. It is also true that this zone would merely turn the clock back to, say, 1950 or the period before massive economic regulation began. Can it be argued that the period before regulation was less safe than the present time?

Overlooked in most calculations of this matter is the purpose behind regulatory bodies. By title and mandate a regulatory body regulates. The Nuclear Regulatory Authority doesn't describe the virtues of nuclear energy; it certainly doesn't advocate the use of an energy source that is generally safe and unthreatening to the environment. It places constraints on this industry. The Environmental Protection Agency doesn't weigh the benefits of an economic reform against the costs of some environmental contamination; it protects the environment. Therefore protection and regulation enter the realm of the sacrosanct and that which encroaches on the environment, even when it improves our lives, is forbidden. Clearly the deck is stacked and as clearly most people intuitively understand this condition.

A "license-free zone" would therefore be the one place the government is removed from the backs of entrepreneurs. It would be New York's answer to Freeport, Maine, the latter a place where you can buy almost anything at a discount. People from all over the world would gravitate to the city to buy products you cannot obtain anywhere else. New York would once again be a commercial hub.

Yet the idea is a serious threat to the status quo. It is a threat to the city commissioners with regulatory responsibility; it is a threat to those who buy into an oligopoly with licenses. In short it threatens the very existence of commercial ventures that depend on restricting competition. Moreover, it threatens those with a stake in retaining poverty. As I see it the "free-licensing zone" should be located in one of the city's poorest areas. It should not only be a mecca for buyers and sellers but for those who want jobs and opportunities. This, after all, is a can't miss proposition. Perhaps more than anything else that is what threatens those wedded to the socialist ethos of big government with great regulatory power. New York can work if people would only remember that this city owes its glorious past to entrepreneurs and economic freedom, not regulators with their sights on a pristine environment and a risk-aversive culture.

September 14, 1986

47

Public-Private Partnership

While there are people who fault Mayor Ed Koch for many things, the one criticism rarely mentioned is the lack of resourcefulness in this city administration for public-private partnerships. Here is a city that rightly or wrongly is considered by many people to be the center of the universe. Yet it is a city whose finances rely disproportionately on two activities: financial services and communication.

For years the city government has neglected a role in promoting economic enterprise. I'm not arguing as most socialists would that the city should be in business. I'm merely advocating a role for the city government in easing the way for business activity and serving as a catalyst for business diversification.

To a minor degree this last point has been understood by the government. In an effort to keep NBC at Rockefeller Center the city offered the blandishment of a major tax abatement. However, tax abatements are handed out by the Koch administration as patronage, a reward for staying in town after threatening to leave. Few people have asked why corporate taxes aren't reduced across the board, especially since the city is in a desperate way to attract new enterprises.

But even more poignant than the city's misguided tax policy is the lack of a practical municipal economic development plan with the city as a major participant. Let me cite several examples of what the city can do that it is not now doing.

For one thing the city could promote middle-class housing by *giving* a developer air rights to municipally owned buildings, e.g., schools, police stations, etc. Since buying a site is the single largest expense in construction, the city could provide these sites gratis if the developer uses this financial windfall as an incentive to keep rentals within the range of middle-class New Yorkers.

For another, the city administration might be a business partner. Suppose the city provides municipal land and a ''no-tax'' arrangement to a developer provided the city becomes a full partner in all profits. This would be an excellent way to develop city property in marginal areas and expand the tax base.

The city could on rare occasions also develop an area when there aren't apparent market reasons for development. For example, the South Bronx could be converted into the garment district, relieving traffic congestion in midtown Manhattan and bring a source of jobs for a region characterized by high unemployment. It makes more sense to spend city funds on a project like this, which may create jobs, than municipal subvention for the poor and unemployed.

It is surprising that in a city that prides itself on resourcefulness, so little is evident in the way economic policies are constructed. In part this may be a function of complacency. Since the mid-1970s when the city neared the brink of bankruptcy, there has been a steady state of congratulations for New York's fiscal health. Despite some steps that improved the city's ledger during these lean years, the Reagan administration more than the Koch administration was responsible for economic vitality in New York. It was the drop in inflation and the surge in investment that rescued the city.

New York is now teetering on the financial brink again. The staggering drop in stock market prices on October 19, 1987 introduced some realism into city financial projections, but the volatile state of the financial services sector has not yet been an incentive for economic diversification. This city is still riding one horse and can't be sure if it will win the Kentucky Derby or be sent to the glue factory.

Public-private partnerships are certainly no panacea for what ails New York. But they do hold out the prospect of something more imaginative and profitable than business as usual. New Yorkers deserve more than they are now getting. It wasn't so long ago that New York was a thriving port, a focus for large and small manufacturing, a textile and furniture center. Those days are gone, but the diversity this description suggests can be recaptured.

There is no justification except tax rates for pharmaceutical companies to be located on the other side of the Hudson. There is no reason why analogue computer firms shouldn't be taking advantage of the technical talent available in New York to advance this budding industry. There is no explanation for bioengineering companies to be largely resident in California instead of New York. What these examples indicate is that the city administration isn't doing enough to promote its own economic interests. If New York's political leaders ignore economic realities, this capital of the world may turn out to be a tourist attraction the way Carthage was a tourist attraction for the Romans.

May 12, 1988

48

Inauthentic Brooklyn Beer

Steven Hindy and Thomas Potter are "suds brothers"; they are, respectively, the president and CEO of the Brooklyn Brewery. Two years ago Steve was the deputy foreign editor at *Newsday* and Tom was a lending officer with Chemical Bank. Although they've been in business for only two years, the company has been selling 3,000 cases of beer a month in its "home" borough. But this is not a story about entrepreneurship. In order to keep costs down, Brooklyn lager is produced in Utica, New York. This superior beer, fermented longer than standard American beers, has a higher malt and hops content and is naturally carbonated.

But any way you look at it, the beer is inauthentic. A Brooklyn beer should be made in Brooklyn. It's bad enough the New York Giants play in New Jersey and the American flag is manufactured in Taiwan. It's disorienting when a New York sirloin steak is better in Kansas City than New York. I wonder how *New York Times* officials feel about their new printing plant in New Jersey. It's worrisome when a New York senator speaks with a Boston accent. But it's downright infuriating when a Brooklyn beer is made in Utica.

I can't blame the owners of the company entirely. After all, production costs are lower in Utica than Brooklyn. But it hurts when the limited partnership that attracted investors is composed largely of New York residents and the bank that offered the biggest loan is the Independence Savings Bank of Brooklyn. There's no justice. What disturbs me is that Brooklyn and the rest of New York aren't considered places to start a new business that sells "New York" products.

How can New York provide incentives so that "our" businesses stay in town? For one thing the mayor's office should realize that New York sells an aura. The name of this city is electric; put it on a label and it sells. You can't do that with Topeka. As a consequence there are an obligation to provide the tax incentives for New Yorkers who wish to start businesses here. If NBC can get a tax break for staying in Rockefeller Center instead of moving to

103

Secaucus, why can't Steve Hindy and Thomas Potter? Selling New York to the world should be a municipal enterprise.

At the moment Brooklyn beer is selling primarily in Brooklyn. But sales have moved across the East River into the Water Club, the Four Seasons, and the American Festival Café. It will soon be selling in D'Agostino's supermarket. And if the principals are smart, they will exploit the name of their lager by taking it to the place where so many Brooklyn people and institutions end up: Los Angeles. Brooklyn is a national state of mind, perhaps the easiest sell Madison Avenue can devise. The rub, of course, is that people who buy Brooklyn products expect authentic Brooklyn products.

Admittedly few products these days are manufactured in the United States. Even the B–1B aircraft depends on Japanese transistors. As an advocate of free trade, I find that there is much to be said for this state of affairs. But it is sheer sacrilege to use the name of Brooklyn for personal gain when the product bearing its name has as much to do with the borough as the Leaning Tower of Pisa. It troubles this former Brooklynite that the dream of residing in this place where a tree grows is being exploited in, of all places, Utica, New York. There was a time when all a comedian had to do to get a laugh was say, "Brooklyn." Phil Foster made a career out of the borough. When the Dodgers left, when the Tip Top sign was taken down, when Steeplechase became a graveyard for rides, the borough seemed to lose its appeal.

But as the sale of Brooklyn lager suggests, there are still people around who remember. This beer isn't sold only because it's good brew. It sells dreams of Jackie dancing off second; of riding the mechanical horses at Steeplechase and eating a hot dog at Nathan's without fear your gold chain will be yanked off. The dreams of New York are for sale, but they should be manufactured in the place that gave birth to them.

To Hindy and Potter I have a message: bring your beer home. Build a brewery in Brooklyn; say goodbye to Utica. Become the Budweiser of Brooklyn, the beer that made the borough famous. Give us brew with authentic labels; manufacture your lager where the dream was born. If the mayor's economic development office won't cooperate, if the banks won't offer loans and the unions won't offer concessions, go public. Offer stock to Brooklyn residents. Give the borough something to dream about again.

November 2, 1988

49

Private Enterprise Responds
to the Bureaucrats

If one wants to develop an understanding of socialism in all its glory, all you have to do is spend one day at the New York City Traffic Department. Unpleasant bureaucrats run the department by the rules and nothing but the rules. The system is unmerciful; an elderly woman and a nineteen-year-old in his Air Jordans are treated the same way. The system is unyielding; "no excuses, get to the back of the line." Here is socialism at work without its supposedly human face. Everyone is indeed treated equally. It also happens to be badly.

Mercifully, our government doesn't control every aspect of our lives. But perhaps more important, it is possible for a free-market system to make government bureaucracies palatable, if not humane. The interstices of government bureaucracy have been filled by private companies who recognize an economic opportunity when they see one.

Civil-service and bar examinations have launched an industry. One can take a test preparation course in order to meet state-mandated standards. The Kaplan bar exam courses and Princeton Review are examples of markets at work. These proprietary schools assist people in meeting standards imposed by a bureaucracy in the name of "credentializing." Without getting into an argument about the veracity of such standards, it is private enterprise that has allowed prospective candidates to obtain state certification by preparing them for the exams.

Similarly, obtaining a passport is one of those nightmares to which most people resign themselves. It is unquestionably an exercise in maintaining one's equilibrium. From the moment you enter this government office till departure, you are herded, abused, and forced to wait. Should you make a mistake in the form, the ultimate penalty awaits you: "Fill out a new form and go to the back of the line." But this state of affairs has been addressed by private services that wait on the line for you. For a fee, other people will be abused, herded, and wait, while you go about your business.

It has also come to my attention that driving schools have hired buses so that their students can be transported to license agencies that aren't so crowded. Officials at these schools take care of every detail associated with obtaining a license. All you have to do is pass the driving test. In New York that is less than half the battle in securing a license.

What these examples indicate is that markets can be created through the deadening experience of dealing with state-sponsored agencies. Alternatives in the economy allow—in fact, promote—enterprise. Beating the system is a noble and profitable act. One can only imagine what life is like when you can't beat the system; when you must wait in line for everything from licenses to toilet paper. This, by the way, is a definition of the Soviet society. Those socialist nations that have loosened the noose of bureaucracy usually mean that someone can be paid off so that the amenities of life may be received. This is the well-understood—if unadvertised—side of socialism, institutional corruption. In most socialist nations you wait on line for the appropriate person to pay off.

It is interesting that as we become more heavily bureaucratized than was ever the case before, private enterprise has carved out a niche for itself as the provider of information and buffer against faceless, insensitive bureaucrats. From my point of view, it would be far better for the society if we had fewer agencies and fewer bureaucrats. But since this condition does not exist, it is a blessing that we have free markets capable of responding to the hazards of bureaucratization.

Of course, some people can't afford to pay for services that allow them to avoid government agencies. That is one of the conditions of free markets. Everyone has the advantage of paying for and receiving a service; but not everyone has the resources to avail himself of that service or recognizes the opportunity costs involved in the calculation. Nonetheless, as a beneficiary of the passport service, I can attest the cost is low, the process efficient, and the time away from the passport office usually well spent. However, even if that time weren't well spent, it was worth the expense to avoid the inevitable migraine headache.

March 12, 1987

Part IV

Social Dimensions of City Life

50

The Human "Time Bombs" on Our Streets

Since 1965 New York State psychiatric hospitals have discharged 73,000 mental patients. The number nationwide can be increased by a factor of four. All but the most severely disturbed have been released, but even in the case of "severely distressed" the intention is often different from the practice. Across the United States these mentally ill people roam the streets. In addition, the psychiatric hospitals have made it difficult for anyone to be admitted. Even deranged people such as the Staten Island ferry-slashing suspect, Juan Gonzalez, remained unhospitalized.

Why this wholesale discharge of mental patients occurred is an interesting story. Mass discharges started for two reasons: the development of "miracle drugs" such as lithium that allow mental patients to live relatively normal lives; and the civil rights movement, which determined that the forced hospitalization of mental patients was a violation of rights—a matter on which many courts agreed.

The problem with these two conditions is that the drugs can affect behavior only if they are taken regularly, and while the civil rights of mental patients may now be protected, public order and safety are often jeopardized as a result.

There are no statistics kept on the number of "deinstitutionalized" patients who commit violent acts after their release. In fact, the percentage may be small. But that does not mitigate the threat to one's safety.

Juan Gonzalez, a homeless Cuban, was known to neighborhood residents as a "weirdo," a person who had conversations with an unaccompanied partner, until he slashed eleven people and killed two on the Staten Island ferry.

Mary Ventura was shuttled in and out of mental hospitals for years. Her state of mind was described by the experts as "stable" until she pushed a woman in front of a subway train.

Another outpatient from Kings County Hospital was arrested for pushing

Renee Katz, a promising flutist, in front of a train. He was acquitted of that crime but recently was arrested for "bumping a woman from behind with his pelvis as a train was approaching."

Even the "experts" on this question and some of the civil rights lawyers recognize the error of their ways. Dr. Steven Katz, New York State mental health commissioner, described deinstitutionalization as "either naivete or poor planning or a combination of both." Dr. Davis Pollack, vice president of the National Alliance for the Mentally Ill, said that, "proper community mental health facilities would help avoid the tragedies like the recent killings on the Staten Island ferry. If there was someone who was making sure he took his medication, it might never have happened."

In most instances, patients are released without any planning. There is usually no discharge plan, no housing plan, and no after-care plan. Patients must fend for themselves, in most cases by finding makeshift shelters in the street. It is interesting to note that money is usually not the issue. In New York state, the Mental Health Department has a $1.8 billion budget with the bulk of that money spent on what is generally recognized as an inefficient bureaucracy.

What is most lacking on this issue is common sense. The deinstitutionalization movement was fatally flawed from the outset. A conviction embraced by a few defied what the average person recognized as an absurd public policy and, incidentally, an inhumane public policy.

The severely mentally ill were not and are not capable of caring for themselves. Wonder drugs are certainly not the answer for those who do not know what day of the week it is, much less the time at which their medication must be taken. Moreover, spaces in mental institutions are available while activists advocate shelters for the "homeless," many of whom are mental patients, recently discharged.

The human time bombs on the streets of our cities are yet another example of the effort of naïve, well-meaning people whose sense of doing good for one group compromises the welfare of everyone else.

There is only one answer for those with mental illness: care in a mental-health facility where medication is given regularly, where beds are available, and where professionals are in attendance. Surely after seeing the "homeless" on the streets of New York, Chicago, Los Angeles, and every major city in this nation, one cannot believe that allowing these wandering urchins to care for themselves is a humanitarian gesture. What the activists with a short memory must do is recall what got us into this fix in the first place. Once they overcome the amnesia, we should be able once again to provide these unfortunate souls with the care they need and deserve.

August 16, 1986

51

The Boggs Affair Revisited

Life is filled with unexpected moments. Several weeks after Joyce Brown, a.k.a. Billie Boggs, spoke at Harvard, telling students about the plight of New York's homeless and excoriating Mayor Koch for "arbitrarily" taking her from the streets because of alleged mental incompetence, Boggs is on the streets yet again. Her New York Civil Liberties Union (NYCLU) lawyer, Norman Siegel, contends that this latest episode of panhandling does not prove Boggs is insane. "Panhandling is not a sign of mental illness," he noted. Nonetheless, Boggs was observed shouting, cursing, and making obscene gestures at passersby and "acting kind of crazy."

What makes this episode so poignant is that Boggs has become something of a celebrity by arguing that the homeless are merely people down on their luck, not those who are deranged. With NYCLU support, the city's right to pick up homeless people from the streets and hold them in mental hospitals against their will was challenged successfully. Brown was freed from a Bellevue psychiatric ward by a judge who ruled the city authorities could not prove she was mentally ill.

If the reports of Boggs's behavior are accurate—and they have been confirmed by several observers—the burden of responsibility rests with the NYCLU and the judge who released her. By using Boggs as a test case these civil libertarians assumed responsibility for her actions once she was released in their custody. However, one suspects Boggs is a pawn in an ever expanding chess game.

The so-called homeless have become one of the big issues on the political landscape. You can always tell what's a big issue by the number of actors who have adopted the cause. The homeless problem has become an actors' bee-hive. Politicians are already on the honey trail. The lamentable part of this activity is that the people who require assistance are largely forgotten in the frenzied political activism.

According to most estimates, about a third of the homeless population is composed of those released from mental institutions, due in large part to the deinstitutionalization movement of the 1970s and '80s. Manic depressives and schizophrenics were handed medication and told to care for themselves. Within a few days, or whenever the medication ran out, these people could be found in the streets mumbling to themselves, accosting pedestrians, and living in their own waste. This policy—if one can dignify it as such—was conducted in the name of humanitarianism.

Presumably psychiatrists could not prove beyond a shadow of a doubt that these released patients are mentally incompetent. After all, even certifiable schizophrenics have lucid moments. As a consequence, it has been argued that freedom cannot be denied, unless mental incompentence can be determined with certainty. Since that cannot be done, the public square has been converted into a squatters zone for many deranged people. To make matters worse, a battery of lawyers representing the civil liberties of those squatters defends their ''right'' to be a scourge on the city.

Billie Boggs is representative of public policy in the grip of ideology. She is by all accounts a woman in desperate need of assistance. But her cause has been transmogrified into a cause célèbre for the homeless. Many people have a stake in seeing her on the streets. These same people have a commitment to claims that she is sane and capable of caring for herself. While this position flies in the face of common sense, common sense has little to do with the Boggs affair.

In my opinion what this case requires is a true custodial relationship. If the NYCLU has people like Boggs released in its custody, then this organization has a responsibility to keep these homeless people off the streets. Norman Siegel can easily demonstrate his good faith by adopting these people as his charge. Instead of simply arranging to have them released in their own recognizance, the NYCLU should assume legal and ethical responsibility for their well-being, as well as assuming some responsibility for the well-being and general welfare of a city significantly affected by the blight of street people.

It is one thing to be a courtroom moralist and quite a different matter to make a genuine commitment to those in need. As far as I can tell, public pronouncements have not done anything to assist the homeless. In fact, if the condition of our streets is any guide, these pronouncements have had a deleterious affect on city life. At the very least the NYCLU has an obligation to explain why Billie Boggs—whose release it arranged—is back on the streets abusing pedestrians, muttering to herself, and being a public nuisance.

April 26, 1988

52

The Web of Civil Libertarian Hypocrisy

On December 3, Joseph Gordon, a thirty-eight-year-old resident of Manhattan, killed a guard at a sporting goods store. Two days earlier the guard had accused Gordon of shoplifting. Gordon, vowing revenge, returned to the store with two knives and in cold blood stabbed the security guard repeatedly through the heart and neck.

When the suspect was apprehended he smiled at the cameras. Both the newspaper picture captions and the New York Civil Liberties Union (NYCLU) assumed this was a "maniacal grin," the expression of a crazed murderer. After all, what rational motive could there be for so heinous a crime? It hasn't occurred to civil liberties lawyers that the planning behind the murder of this security guard probably could not have been accomplished by an insane person.

At the same time this incident was unfolding, the NYCLU was protesting the city's efforts to take a street woman, called Billie Boggs, to Bellevue Hospital against her will. The NYCLU contended that even though Boggs lived over a hot-air vent on East 65th Street, she was not insane and her rights were violated by the involuntary pickup. The fact that she lived in her own excrement, burned money, exploded at passersby for no apparent reason did not seem to be evidence of mental incompetence for NYCLU lawyers.

These two cases put the longstanding hypocrisy of the civil liberties movement clearly in focus. Murderers, on the very evidence of their heinous crimes, are insane and therefore should not be treated as mentally competent in a court of law. On the other hand, street people—even those living in human waste—can never be thought of as insane even though they cannot care for themselves and are a blight on our city.

Under these conditions the average person who expects to live in relative safety and cleanliness cannot win. The murderer will in most cases be released in two or three years to commit further crimes. Is it any wonder Joseph Gordon was smiling at the moment of apprehension? On the other hand, the homeless—a scourge on our streets—cannot be given the care and treatment institutionalization can provide. What these combined conditions represent is an urban area neither safe, clean, nor humane. In fact, in the name of civil liberties, life in our cities is brutalized.

In my judgment sensible people should require civil libertarians to make a clear and forthright claim about insanity. Either mental incompetence exists or it does not. If the former, then it is quite appropriate to hospitalize street people involuntarily. If the latter, then mental incompetence as a defense for murder is inapplicable. But as things now stand, lawyers, backed up by the NYCLU, can have their cake and eat it too.

An increase in violent crime is due in some part to the recognition by criminals that with plea bargaining, crowded prisons, early parole, and the insanity defense, most murderers serve no more than a few years in the slammer. Is it any wonder that so many inner-city youths carry illegal weapons? Or that many of them smile when they are caught? The result of all our measures to diminish the likelihood of punishment is the fear of violence that permeates the ambience of the city.

Yet despite the expectations, despite the barbarism, despite the fear that exists among law-abiding citizens, despite the record, civil libertarian lawyers continue to spin a web of rights-generated precedents that release murderers in their own recognizance and allow the mentally incompetent to befoul our streets and brutalize themselves.

While the recently labeled "homeless people" represent a diverse population of those down on their luck, a criminal element, drug users, and alcoholics, there is little question that a substantial number of these people are those once described as mentally incompetent. With the deinstitutionalization movement of the 1970s, many in this category were released from mental-care units and forced to look after themselves in hallways and alcoves, and over heating vents. It is inaccurate to suggest we have more vagrants today, but it is accurate to argue they are more visible than was the case in the past. In our desire to restore the civil liberties of those held against their will, we have converted our cities into open sewers and brutalized those people we claim to be helping.

Clearly Joseph Gordon and Billie Boggs are not the same person. Their public offenses are very different. Yet each is a symbol in the civil liberties controversy. If Gordon is released after his cold-blooded murder, no one can be safe on our streets. If Billie Boggs is released to her hot-air vent on 65th Street, further squalor in our cities and a lack of humanity must be expected.

December 29, 1987

53

New York's Forgotten People

In the last few months the chilling horror of youthful beatings and murder has filled the pages of New York's newspapers. There was the incident in Howard Beach, the attempted incineration of hoboes in Prospect Park, the murder of a high school football star in Ozone Park, and the unprovoked beating of three black youths in Canarsie. What each of these horrible crimes has in common is that the assailants are white.

On the face of it, this shouldn't be an issue. Everyone knows that crime doesn't discriminate. There have always been white, brown, black, yellow, and red criminals. However, in recent years, as Police Commissioner Ward has noted, most serious crimes in this city are committed by youthful black offenders. Those who speak about inner-city crime invariably use "inner city" as a code for blacks.

Knowledge of the "inner city" and its well-advertised crime has prompted various reform proposals. There's the cry for new public housing. There is the now common call for recreational facilities. There are the job-training programs. While none of these efforts specifically employs race as a criterion for participation, it is obvious to any dispassionate observer that these government programs are designed ostensibly to assuage black opinion.

That, in fact, is how our political system has come to function. But there is another minority in our city left out of these antipoverty efforts. In fact, these are the forgotten people who aren't even mentioned in sociological treatises. These people are inner-city white residents who don't have the resources to move to the suburbs. They live side by side with blacks and Hispanics, but are almost never mentioned as part of the city's problems.

Recent events, however, suggest we had better recognize these white ethnics as part of the problem. Low representation on the criminal rolls doesn't tell the whole story. Poverty, poor housing, a lack of recreational facilities afflict whites as well as blacks. Moreover, the important difference between whites and blacks in this city is that the white problems aren't

115

recognized. They have been made invisible by the definition of the urban dilemma.

This is not to suggest that the behavior of these white assailants can be excused because of social conditions or that one can generalize from this small sample. Living in brand-new houses rarely affects the crime rate. What I'm getting at is that white ethnics have been defined out of urban problems, despite the deep-seated pathology that often exists in this community.

In the 1920s and 1930s the reverse was the case. During those decades "the East Side Kids" was a metaphor for urban delinquents. There was certainly black crime, although the rate was lower than at present, but blacks were defined out of the urban malaise. There didn't appear to be enough of them in cities to constitute a problem. Yet the numbers game has its drawbacks.

When unemployed white thugs in Canarsie beat up black kids for no other reason but their race, something is desperately wrong. Surely bigotry is not new; its ugly face resurfaces periodically in this city. But the spate of serious crimes committed by white youngsters should make all New Yorkers pause. Criminality is not restricted to one race. Nor should efforts to eliminate its causes be restricted to one race.

It's time for politicians to realize that they must do more than respond reflexively to the plea for additional aid for urban blacks. There are others in this town who suffer from poverty, broken homes, a lack of purpose, the drug contagion, and the other characteristics associated with crime. These white ethnics are fast becoming the latest crime statistic. It is not entirely surprising, but it is disturbing, particularly since social descriptions of the last few decades have converted this population into an invisible people.

October 7, 1987

54

Assault in the Subway

For any New Yorker who uses the subway on a regular basis there is the anticipation of terror, that moment when, like Bernhard Goetz, one may be accosted by thugs. Examples abound. But there are actually very few reports on another omnipresent condition in the subways: the assault on one's sensibilities. These are the unreported, noncriminal events that occur each day and are within the experience of every subway rider.

To prove this point I asked several women to tell me about incidents they have experienced using the subway on a regular basis.

One woman, taking the IRT Broadway line from 125th Street to 72nd Street, reports that on one recent mid-afternoon sojourn in which she was alone on the last car of the train, a man exposed himself. He didn't make any hostile gestures, but it was clear he was exposing himself to her.

Another respondent told me that at the 42nd Street and Seventh Avenue station near the BMT lines, a vagrant positioned himself in a steel frame revolving door while defecating.

Still another mentioned the addicts and drunks who routinely take over several seats on the "F" train from Manhattan to Continental Avenue while sleeping off their drug-induced stupor.

My wife told me about a fellow who shadow-boxes on the East Side IRT line even when the train car is filled with people. He doesn't hit anyone, but then again he has a space all to himself.

An elderly woman who uses the BMT regularly noted that despite restrictions on cigaret smoking, there are smokers on her car without fail. She happens to be allergic to smoke, but wouldn't dare ask these people to observe the law.

Yet another woman noted that the stairwell between the Sixth and Eighth Avenue lines at the Fourth Street IND station is an open urinal. Not only is the stench abominable, but those urinating can be observed almost any evening.

One woman, who takes the IRT line from Brooklyn to Manhattan each morning, points out the panhandlers who generally board the train at the 14th Street station. Each one has a story. There is the Vietnam veteran unable to obtain his military benefits; the mother and infant daughter who are not yet on the welfare rolls; the disabled person who desperately needs spare change. A cup is flung in the rider's face, despite her attempt to hide behind a newspaper.

There is really no way to avoid the assault. But most sensible New York subway riders try. Averting one's eyes is a common technique. It is a rare occasion when anyone makes eye contact on the subway, even during the rush hour when one is made to feel like a goose being stuffed for pâté. Most people bring reading material on the trains in an effort to insulate themselves from the sensual barrage. Subway riders all wear psychological blinders.

Despite these learned responses to the subway's appalling conditions, daily rides take their toll. "When I'm on the trains I turn into a zombie; I don't look at anyone," said one young woman. Another maintains that "Any human feeling, any sentiment, has been drummed out of me in the subway. I'm two people—one who rides the subway and one who responds to the rest of the world."

These are reactions to events the police would describe as "nuisance issues." Yet they are also a ubiquitous aspect of subway riding. That is the point overlooked by the many policy analysts who concentrate exclusively on subway crime. If all the crime could be magically eliminated tomorrow, the subway experience would still be an assault on the average rider.

Most regular riders—as opposed to those people who use the trains periodically—are inured to the sounds, smells, and vulgarities on the trains. They know what to expect. These people are a special breed; they are tougher, more adaptable, infinitely more patient than taxi riders. They are, in fact, the real New Yorkers.

Yuppies don't recognize them and limousine liberals don't identify with them. But that hardly matters. These people emerge from the bowels of the earth each day to earn a living. By the time they reach a desk, they have endured more hardship than the typical executive tolerates in a year. These are heroes in our midst. I wish that something could be done to help them.

July 7, 1987

55

The Absurdity of Distributing
Needles to Addicts

New York City administrators have decided to distribute clean needles to intravenous drug users in order to combat the spread of AIDS. Although this decision is a reversal of earlier deliberations, state officials have decided to allow distribution of clean needles to hundreds of drug addicts in the first stage of an experiment that would ultimately be expanded to include thousands of users.

Approved by state Health Commissioner David Axelrod, the city's plan would be operated through the New York City Health Department and presumably would be suspended if the spread of AIDS through shared-needle use is not diminished.

John Cardinal O'Connor expressed the sentiment of many of the plan's critics by noting, "It drags down the standards of all society." Clearly the moral value of sanctioning drug use through a city-sponsored, hypodermic-needle-distribution program is perverse on its face. Moreover, even on a pragmatic level there is no way of knowing whether these city-distributed needles will be shared by drug users, thereby spreading the disease this program is designed to curb.

But with very few exceptions the critics have not taken note of what happens when the government gives anything away. It is not coincidental that the blankets given to the so-called homeless are now sold at open bazaars in many city locations or that city-distributed methadone is sold by addicts to other addicts. Might not there be an underground market for the sale of government-distributed needles?

Give-away programs of this kind are invariably fraught with unanticipated problems. Drug companies severely restricted by law will be forced into the unethical practice of distributing hypodermic needles. With needles distributed freely, there will be those who claim that the quality is below par and the quantity is restricted. These are the proverbial claims that can be made for any government-sponsored program.

It is almost inescapable that a suit will be brought against the state for promoting drug use or, if an addict dies of an overdose after using drugs in a hypodermic needle, charges of manslaughter. It is also probable that if this program becomes part of the landscape of government-assistance activities, at some time in the future there will be a needle-procurement kickback scandal with a politician indicted for taking a bribe.

None of these conditions is assured; they are, however, part of a history anyone familiar with give-away programs knows. Yet the obsession with AIDS has forced government officials to act in a manner that is unethical and unreasonable. One could easily argue that the way to decrease the AIDS contagion among drug addicts is to prevent the use of drugs. If the at-risk population can infect newborns and others, the liberty of addicts to use drugs with needles of any kind may have to be restricted.

So far along the road to relativism have we gone as a culture, that promoting one evil to stamp out a problem is considered an appropriate public-policy response. Officials weigh the relative evils in society unmindful of the effect government-sanctioned programs have on those who abuse the law and often abuse themselves. The message in this needle-distribution program is clear: an AIDS epidemic has forced health officials into the indefensible position of promoting drug use willy-nilly.

Even if one rejects the moral argument against needle distribution, there is still the irrationality of yet another government give-away program that is inherently inefficient. The additional cost of several pennies for clean needles to drug users who spend several dollars getting high, is not unreasonable. If drug users wish to survive—a highly dubious proposition in the first place— the investment of several pennies for clean needles shouldn't be an exorbitant price to pay, nor should it be the responsibility of government to provide them. The next thing you know the government will provide everything from the "nickel bag" to the needle so that it can be confident the drug abuser hasn't contracted AIDS. Where does one draw the line?

It is precisely on this point that government programs have failed. State officials don't know where to draw the line. A needle inserted into the bloodstream for a high is also a spear inserted into the soul of a nation. Governments simply don't know how to deal with these matters efficiently and they often overlook the ethical consequences of their actions.

February 13, 1988

56

The Homosexual "Live for Today" Childless Vision

Members of the Riverside Church, already well known for their pro-Sandinista position, approved a pro-gay policy that accepts homosexuality as part of an extended definition of Christian family life. The Reverend William Sloan Coffin argued that henceforth the church will accept homosexuals as full members of this Christian brotherhood. A policy statement notes: "We recognize and embrace single persons, lesbians [and] gay relationships, extended families and all families of support that are founded on principles of love and justice."

While the Coffin proposal was accepted by the majority of church members present, it did face rigorous opposition. Reverend Channing Phillips argued that homosexuality deviates from biblical teaching, since heterosexuality was virtually ordained by the book of Genesis.

Whether homosexuality is a sin because it deviates from the book of Genesis is a matter over which theologians will dispute. What is not in dispute is the anti-Christian logic of a family that will not, cannot procreate. To deny the family the opportunity to sustain the species is a contradiction in terms. There is no biblical prescription or Judeo-Christian tradition on which homosexuality can rest, since its opposition to the sustenance of the species is antithetical to survival, and as a consequence in opposition to the basis of Christianity.

No matter how open or humane this church tries to be, it cannot deny this contention. Joseph Schumpeter made the point that the homosexual's "childless vision" militates against a commitment to the social order. After all, society's stability is predicated on a vision of the future. One buys life insurance for children, and defends a nation for generations to come. The homosexual by necessity forecloses on the future. Is it not coincidental, argues Schumpeter, that John Maynard Keynes was a homosexual. His theory of economics emphasized consumption and virtually ignored savings. Is it possible that Keynes, like many homosexuals, adopted in his economic theory a "live for today" attitude because he was uninterested in the future?

The currently faddish attempt to incorporate aberrational behavior into the mainstream loses sight of the fact that homosexuals are not committed to the continuation of this social order. I am not suggesting that they are necessarily unpatriotic or disloyal. What I do contend is that there is an unwillingness to defend the present system for an unrealizable future.

While defenders of the homosexual position contend that the society requires openness to accommodate all "lifestyles"—a word I abhor—on one matter they have been decidedly closemouthed: defending the future. Where, it might be asked, are the defenders of future generations? Are they to be found residing in the fringe environmental groups who worry about endangered species like the snail darter but ignore human existence?

Certainly the tolerance of different views is one measure of civility. But it does no one any good, including its supposed beneficiaries, to suggest that aberrational sexuality is normal or Christian or socially acceptable. This does not mean that homosexuals should face discrimination or censure. The extent of the Fifth and Fourteenth amendments should apply to homosexuals as they do for the rest of us. However, the stand taken by the Riverside Church is unjustified by religious doctrine or common sense. The only thing that can be said for it is that the position is compatible with the church's view of nuclear weapons, Latin American policy, arms negotiations with the Soviets, capitalism's flaws, and liberality toward criminals in this city. One can always count on the Reverend Mr. Coffin to take absurd stands on public-policy issues. Once again he hasn't disappointed.

June 13, 1985

57

Cultural Bias and Tests for the Police

A coalition of black police officers and psychologists recently made a formal statement in which they decried psychological tests as "culturally biased: and an obstacle to police jobs." While charges against civil-service exams are common, this is the first time—to my knowledge—that a psychological test was castigated as biased.

According to Gerald Horne, director of the National Conference of Black Lawyers—one of the organizations in the coalition—"only two of the over 800 questions on the test deal specifically with race and racism." The concerns about the testing were among the preliminary findings of a five-month study of the police force prompted by allegations of brutality aimed at blacks.

Dr. Eloise Archibald, director for the New York City psychological testing unit, said 22 percent of black applicants between February and December 1985 had been disqualified after psychological testing, compared with 17 percent of Hispanic applicants and 12 percent of white applicants.

This one-year sample seemed to confirm her experience since 1979. Several studies have found that blacks tend to get scores in an "unacceptably high" range for depression and mania. This result in itself does not invalidate the Minnesota Multiphasic Psychological Inventory usually employed for such testing.

It might be useful to discover why blacks have an inclination to exhibit depression or mania, but on the face of it the condition rather than the exam appears to be the problem. However, the contention of bias in a psychological test raises disturbing questions. If psychological tests discriminate against black applicants to a police department, how can sociopaths be identified and withdrawn from the pool of police candidates? After all, it is a response to police brutality that prompted the investigation in the first place.

This issue is also complicated by the arguments surrounding affirmative action. Presumably the special attention given minority applicants for a job is related to the psychological stress their status has caused in a predominantly white society. That may be a dubious point but it is the basis for affirmative action. It should therefore not be surprising when black applicants have higher than average scores in depression and mania.

If the psychological test results are invalid, there is probably no argument for affirmative action. Conversely, if affirmative action is needed there is reason to believe blacks will score at unacceptable levels on psychological tests. But you can't have it both ways. If one discards civil service exams as biased and now psychological tests for the same reason, selection will be based on a first-come, first-served basis through strict quotas or a throw of the dice.

However, if these are methods of selection, there may be no way to prevent police brutality or for that matter aberrational behavior of any kind.

In lobbying for a special interest, namely black police officers, this coalition of organizations has overlooked the segment of our population most affected by crime and police brutality: blacks.

Instead of describing screening devices as culturally biased, these groups should be actively seeking screens that protect their own people from abuse. Tests don't measure the person. That is common sense. But it is also common sense to argue that some measure of the person is necessary. One gets the impression from these complaints about applicant procedures that any screening method eliminating black applicants will be found culturally biased.

It is a tribute to this nation that concerns such as racial bias are taken seriously. It is also an inverted form of racism to proclaim bias whenever the results of an exam fail to fit your view of the world. There are indeed racists who should be excoriated. There are also racial rationalists who should be excoriated. Establishing fairness in employment practices isn't easy.

It might surprise some black organizations to learn that the ally in this matter of fairness is tests. A score doesn't measure the color of one's skin. Nor does it tell us who is most able to handle the responsibility of being a cop. But it is a start and it's also better than the spoils system.

July 15, 1986

58

Ethnic Stereotyping Comes with the Territory of Rights for Minorities

The American Museum of Natural History has canceled a lecture series entitled "Ethnic Communities of New York" because museum administrators decided that the description of ethnic groups in the brochure announcing the events could be construed as offensive.

According to the museum's manager, the ethnic descriptions were "in dubious taste." For example, the description of Italians reads: "San Gennaro, the Godfather and the Black Hand, the importance of garlic." A description of Orthodox Jews includes the words "The Chosen, keeping the Sabbath, scholarship, dairy restaurants, the ghetto."

The museum manager of public affairs said, "The problem was simply one of bad editing." He maintained that the lectures should have dealt with the evils of stereotypes. But if one is to study ethnic groups, what emerges are types. In the current climate of opinion the difference between a type and a stereotype is a difference without a distinction.

When one considers that the fallout of the civil rights movement was the expression of ethnic assertiveness that had formerly been submerged, it is not at all surprising that the search for what is unique has led to the shoals of ethnic stereotyping. This is truly a case of being hoisted by one's petard. The activists who wanted an expression of idiosyncratic characteristics are embarrassed by the superficial generalizations that emerge with ethnic identification. In fact the categories of people are generalizations. It is simply tautological to argue that Italians eat Italian food or Orthodox Jews study the Old Testament.

Museum officials may attempt to couch brochures in less offensive language, but the language of groups is necessarily stereotyping. If one argues that some Chinese are influenced by Confucius, the statement may be indisputable, but it is not a description of an ethnic group. Some Americans, Koreans, and Malaysians are influenced by Confucius too. It is the categorical claims that comprise ethnic studies. Individuals are melted in the cauldron of group identification.

Before the 1960s, even before the claims of "unmeltable ethnics," the relationship between filial piety and loyalty to one's adopted home was understood. Assimilation was an accommodation between old and new. The strains between them were mitigated by mutual tolerance. Italians march on Fifth Avenue to celebrate Columbus's discovery of America, but have volunteered in large numbers to fight for their adopted home even when it meant fighting against the land of their birth.

When it became fashionable to ignore loyalty to the United States, ethnic ties became paramount. The sensitive relationship that permitted the love of old and new surrendered to an exaggerated fascination with a world that was a faint if apotheosized memory and to a taking for granted of the home that provided prosperity and freedom.

This evolution marked a significant departure from the stated national goal of assimilation, even though that goal was honored as much in the breach as in practice. With 1960s activists the illusions were shattered. Young people sought to disinter memories—often inaccurate memories—of another time and place. Even WASPs were perceived as an ethnic group. Ethnicity came to rule the academic kingdom. New courses were offered in large part to satisfy the political demands for Balkanization. In fact, most of the courses were an invention. The liberal ethos of individual will was replaced by categories—women, blacks, Hispanics, white ethnics. It is hardly surprising that the upshot of this development is stereotyping.

The irony of the present condition is that the unleashing of ethnic concerns appears as a "boiled-down" portrait of national, religious, and racial groups deemed to be of "dubious taste." Curiously, the ethnic revolution was victorious but the victory was pyrrhic. Now that people emphasize their ethnic backgrounds, we are sensitive to group depictions.

But can one describe the New York East Indians without referring to saris, the Sacred Cow, and newspaper stands? Can one discuss Harlem blacks without reference to jazz, civil rights, fried chicken, and caste? If these characteristics are perceived as superficial—which they are—then what is the meaning of limning the ethnic experience? What is a group portrait except the few traits that distinguish one group from another, very often traits of the lowest common denominator?

That officials at the Museum of Natural History chose to cancel a series of ethnic lectures is not surprising. Surely these officials should have known that with the lid taken off ethnicity, anything can be said, including the obvious portrayal of collective traits. Stereotyping may be embarrassing to some, but that is what ethnic studies have become.

March 18, 1986

Part V

Crime

59

One Victim's Encounter with
the Criminal Justice System

My saga with the criminal justice system began in April of this year. Like most New Yorkers, I have not been affected by crime directly, but I know it's around. I see the drug deals on the streets, the petty theft, and occasionally the major crimes. But I naïvely felt insulated.

I use the past tense because in April my wife's pocketbook was stolen with almost all of our possessions—a substantial amount of cash (it was pay day), our savings book, checkbook, and credit cards (every one under God's prosperous sun).

With alacrity we notified the credit card companies, canceled our outstanding checks, and informed the manager of our local bank. Yet even though we did all of this in the first two hours after the robbery, the thieves were faster. They had managed to get $300 in cash with the Master Charge card, clothes with the Bloomingdale's card, gasoline with the Mobil card, and came within a hair's breadth of cleaning out our savings account.

Moreover, they are aware of the fact that no retailer examines purchases under $25. Needless to say, our liability is restricted. But try telling that to a retailer who just cashed one of your recently stolen checks. Try to explain to the credit department at Bloomingdale's that the $24 purchase of nightgowns isn't yours. In fact try to explain anything to the credit department at Bloomingdale's.

The anguish and embarrassment drove me to distraction. My wife and I wandered through the streets where the robbery took place hoping she could identify the thieves.

In late August, however, we received notification from the 44th Precinct in the Bronx that someone using our Mobil card had been apprehended.

By September we were asked to appear in Bronx Criminal Court as witnesses against the defendant. The defendants, who were young and black, sat on the left side of the court, joking around, reading newspapers, and seeming to be quite at ease; witnesses, like us, sat on the right side, obviously tense and nervous.

Finally, our case was brought before the judge. I leaned forward in anticipation of his judgment. The defendant in question was charged with his third offense, but he seemed as relaxed as I do when engaged in biofeedback.

My wife and I eagerly asked the assistant district attorney assigned to the case what he would get. The assistant district attorney shuffled through some papers and then said, "Third offense? He'll get three years of probation."

"What does that mean?" I inquired. "Will he be fined? Jailed?"

"No," he replied. "He'll be on probation for three years. If he commits another crime, he'll be in *real* trouble."

I looked at this young fellow, gritted my teeth, and said, "You are inaccurate in your assessment. He won't be in trouble if he commits another crime, he'll be in trouble if he's caught."

My wife and I left the courtroom observing the jocularity and relaxed mood of the defendants. It was now easier for us to understand their attitude. We came to the court seeking justice; we left knowing a little better how justice is served.

October 5, 1981

60

Daytime Barbarism on a Midtown Subway

Last week I entered the 33rd Street East Side IRT station at 2:15 P.M. Although I ride the subways somewhat regularly, this was the first time in several years that I found myself in a station during a nonrush hour and at a time when youths are leaving school. Approximately seventy-five students from Norman Thomas High School entered the station at the same time I did.

The first thing I observed is that not one of these students put a token in the turnstile or showed a pass; they either jumped over the barrier or walked through the emergency door. A change dispenser looked at me with a combination of remorse and resignation. He had obviously experienced this scene before. Pandemonium prevailed, fights broke out, obscenities were shouted, jostling ensued.

When the train arrived, these students rushed toward every available seat. A young man wearing a San Antonio Spurs jacket stretched his legs out on the bench, taking up at least three seats. Once the train started to move almost everyone took out a hero sandwich and soda. In an instant the car was transformed into a lunchroom. Food was thrown across the car and bottles and cans were strewn about. One black woman handed a can to one of the students, saying, "This belongs to you. Throw the bottle in a receptacle, thank you."

When the student got off at the 14th Street station he stood behind a pillar until the door closed and the train started. As the train inched forward slowly he hurled the empty soda bottle through the open window at the woman who had chastised him, narrowly missing her head.

The car was empty of students at this point, but their presence was still felt. Empty bottles and bags were on the floor and seats. One half-filled bottle of Welch's grape soda left on the floor spilled its syrupy liquid at every stop and start. As soon as the liquid started to dry, its stickiness could be felt underfoot.

This is not a story of physical abuse, although in the case of one woman that was intended. But there is no question this was an assault on one's sensibilities. For only four stops or roughly eight minutes there wasn't the slightest adherence to civilized behavior in that train car. Here were the new barbarians who simply took over the subway car without the slightest regard for their fellow passengers.

Clearly the lack of respect was not due to abuse that was leveled against these students, nor could one explain it with the commonly employed reliance on poverty. These kids were well dressed in satin jackets, Puma sneakers, and designer jeans. They simply did not care what kind of impression they were making. They were unschooled in the most rudimentary social skills.

As I climbed the stairs out of the subway I thought about the fundamental need for civility in a setting where the crush of people is apparent. Without civil behavior, the gossamer-thin social control that keeps barbarism in check is torn to shreds. People cannot live in an urban setting without some acceptance of civil accord.

It is absurd to think that social harmony can emerge from the expression of licentious behavior. Those who argue that adolescents are going through a rebellious stage in which they find a need to express themselves ignore the consequences of that claim. If one can excuse uncivilized behavior, one can excuse anything.

It is not an irrational leap to go from the scene I've described on a subway to unlawful behavior on the streets. If the prevailing view of some adolescents is to act in a manner that brings personal pleasure at the risk of pain to others, the only inhibition is external restraint. Where that doesn't exist, the average person is a pawn to be influenced by the whims of tormentors. That is the horror of uncivilized behavior. For eight minutes I found myself in its grip. It is not a pleasant experience, but it is probably one most New Yorkers have endured.

May 2, 1985

61

How I Learned to Respect the Police: Notes of a Civilian Observer

As a boy, I used to put on the policeman's cap I was given as a birthday present and daydream about catching a thief. I was preserving law and order against the onslaught of criminal offenders. "John Dillinger stick 'em up, ya under arrest." I never really outgrew these fantasies, although as I was passing through a postadolescent Marxist phase in my life, the police became the enemy. That was very temporary, however, a little like the period when I believed that I would be president of the United States.

In the 1960s my affection for policemen was rediscovered. Despite what I read about police brutality at Columbia University and Berkeley, California, I observed an extraordinary degree of self-restraint and professional behavior exhibited by the police under the most trying circumstances. How would you like to be called "pig" by hundreds of angry teenagers for doing your assigned job or have dog feces thrown at you for asking some ersatz Lenin to take his feet off the university president's desk?

As a police sympathizer, my passions may have been with the law officers, but as an academic I discussed criminal matters with all the dispassion a scholar can muster. My students, of course, did not appreciate the dispassionate analysis and actively resisted the passionate claims. However, I did admit that my experience was limited and my arguments were distillations of secondary sources. That was something I lamented, but, no matter what I wished, my childish daydreams remained unfulfilled and my knowledge vicarious.

This condition was to change more quickly than I could have imagined. It started when the New York Council of the Humanities funded a project to have humanists (academics, journalists, and religious leaders) ride with police officers and discuss police issues. I was selected as one of these humanists. Unbeknownst to my benefactors, I was secretly longing to sacrifice my books for a patrol car. What I craved was to be a knight in blue, fulfilling atavistic yearnings.

The police, I discovered, are not what my daydreams were about, nor are they the sensational subjects most newspaper reporters tend to highlight. They are unquestionably caught in the maelstrom of urban decay they did not create. They have an impossible job that the citizenry generally does not understand and is often unwilling to support. Now that the obvious is noted, it should be pointed out that most of these men are brave and decent, although some simply do "the job" and a small number are psychopathic and brutal. It amazes me that some policemen can say, "I'll make a collar at 11:00 P.M." and do it every time. Is that chance or a result of the use of provocation to bolster one's arrest record?

What is also interesting is that, while most reporters discuss the stress on the job, few realize that the stress police complain about most emanates from petty and arbitrary decisions made by politicians who use the crime problem for their own purposes.

These random thoughts were not learned through a couple of scatter-shot visits to the Bronx, my assignment area—I worked with a team in the Bronx Taskforce and rode in their patrol car for forty hours over a two-month period. Admittedly, that does not qualify me as an expert, albeit John Kenneth Galbraith knows less about China than I know about the Bronx and that certainly did not stop him from writing a book about the subject.

My first day at the Bronx Taskforce office was revealing. The officers in this unit think of themselves as an elite command that has the mobility to address any trouble spot in the borough. The esprit is obvious. A pastel drawing of a skull and crossbones with a police cap serves as the unit symbol. The walls have *New York Daily News* headlines with handwritten supplements: e.g., "The T.F. cares for the aged"; "Keep the faith, make a collar today." There are statistics of arrests from January 1 to the present. The conversation is sprinkled with references to children, being overweight, and an anticipated softball game. An outsider would feel quite confident in asserting that these cops share some special camaraderie.

I was assigned to two officers who have been with the Taskforce for several years. They are seasoned professionals who are glib, tough, sensitive, bright, and as easy to talk to as anyone I have ever known. Despite some initial apprehension in their response to me, I actually looked forward to our conversation as much as to my chance to experience police work. These men could talk knowledgeably about chess, child-rearing, pop music, Arthur Jensen's theories of genetics and intelligence, Dr. J. (basketball star Julius Erving), and police behavior. They stared long and hard at well-built women and smiled easily at children. They are not especially gung-ho about their work, but, if we found ourselves in a difficult situation, I was happy to know they were on my side.

They know the streets the way I know my classroom. Relatively trivial matters that might suggest something is awry were usually noticed. "I wonder why the birds are so active in that particular tree?" "Those kids don't look as if they belong on that school bus." They have street savvy that lets their minds filter events the way screens distinguish between sand and solid objects.

The fact that they are black is important. It was difficult to ride more than a half a mile without their waving to someone they know. I often thought that half the Bronx must be related to these men. Moreover, by knowing and caring about so many, they become neighborhood cops in the only way that expression makes sense.

On my first day out, we rode through the 4–6, an area in transition that is feeling the cancerous effects of South Bronx sprawl. It is interesting that the South Bronx, which used to be the area between 130th and 138th streets, now encompasses every part of the Bronx up to Yankee Stadium. Buildings with lovely façades are abandoned and mangy dogs stand vigil in front of apartments that their owners left months ago. This area combines some stable families, the elderly—too poor to migrate to Miami—and transients, who comprise the bulk of the criminal element.

Fordham Road, smack in the center of this precinct, is still a mecca for shoppers. Old women, who have made a ritualistic walk along the Grand Concourse till they reach the Bronx's most famous bargain emporium, Alexander's Department Store, can still be found with babushkas on their heads, rolled-down Supphose stockings, and old woolen coats that cover the calf. There is one striking difference, however, between the past and now—fear. These women are the bait for fourteen- and fifteen-year-old "juveniles" eager to make a fast buck. At times these teenagers use knives for their larceny, sometimes a tug is sufficient, and some even employ attack dogs. The effect is the same. Everyone is scared, but the walkers are out because they would not know what else to do with their lives.

As we were riding about four blocks south of Fordham Road on what was a very peaceful day, "my partners" (Scotty and Kenny)—I was obviously getting deep into my role—stopped the car in front of a street scene that included an unconscious woman, a man trying to prop her up and occasionally slap her into consciousness, and several very youthful spectators. Scotty bent down over her, held her hand gently, and mumbled some inaudible words. Miraculously, she woke up. Flailing at her boyfriend, she shouted for all of the Bronx to hear that she was the sister of the Black Jesus. That condition— she alleged—had caused all her problems. It was obvious that the woman was drugged or deranged.

We drove her to the hospital at breakneck speed only after Scotty promised he would not leave her side. She seemed to know every nurse at the hospital and most of the doctors. "Where is Dr. Greenspan?" she bellowed. "He's the only one who understands me.'' The nurse asked Scotty about the case, but all he said was ''She should be detoxified.'' Apparently, if he claimed she required psychiatric assistance, he would have had to spend the entire day talking to psychiatrists before a decision about her future would be made. It was far simpler to avoid that issue.

After that scene, I started to understand the policeman's role a little better. He is part social worker, part psychologist, and peripherally a crime fighter. When he is on the beat or parks his car, he becomes a willy-nilly police department. He makes decisions about when to arrest, when to ignore, and when to assist. That kind of responsibility takes its toll, especially when command decisions invariably resemble ''Catch-22.'' For example, at one meeting the men in the Taskforce were told to ''keep up the numbers''— translation: more arrests and summonses. The same commander, however, said that in Co-op City (a huge complex of high-rise apartment houses, in itself larger than many U.S. cities) there were to be no summonses given out at all. Now how does a police officer ''keep up the numbers'' if he is assigned to Co-op City? That kind of contradictory direction has its effect. Moreover, if the newspapers discover an issue, so will the command. There is no police initiative—the men are told to respond to what the press has discovered. Crimes against the elderly only became an issue when the *New York Post* ran a special series on the matter. Experienced officers can predict their assignments on the basis of newspaper headlines.

One spring day, as Kenny, Scotty, and I were involved in an animated conversation about the impending basketball playoffs, a well-dressed guy stopped the car on Westchester Avenue and angrily said, ''Some kid holding a gun in his hand said he was goin' to blow my head off.'' He pointed in the direction the youth was walking. We drove quickly along Westchester Avenue in the wrong direction until we approached a male seventeen-to-twenty-year-old who held what appeared to be a revolver in his right hand. Scotty and Kenny jumped out of the car in an instant. Kenny ran directly up to him from behind as Scotty negotiated his way around a row of parked cars. They moved like two football defensive backs, each compensating for the other's moves. I stood back, nervous about what would happen. Would the youth be ''blown away''? Would he instinctively turn and start firing before Kenny reached him? I stood frozen for several seconds as adrenalin pumped through my body. When I next looked up, Kenny had his hand on the gun and the youth was disarmed. It turned out to be a plastic pistol.

''Did you know that was a toy gun?'' I asked. ''No,'' Kenny replied. ''I simply wanted to close the distance between us as fast as possible. I didn't know that was a toy until I got my hand on it.'' Kenny and Scotty understand the street scene and one another so well that their reaction time was phenomenal. Before my heartbeat could adjust to events, the matter was over.

The danger in police activity is palpable. What generally is not known—

partly because of television programming—is the sheer boredom of the job. Riding in a squad car for eight hours on a day shift with no reports from Central Headquarters can be deadly. There are women to look at on the streets and talk about their children's Little League game. There is a rating system on female anatomy and Italian pastry—anything to make the time go faster.

Occasionally, there is humor. In an area overheated with tension, that is one of the few releases. On one tour, our car was hailed by a cab driver. In a thick Yiddish accent, he told us that a woman was trying to "stiff him" for $10. A Columbia University professor had taken this cab from Manhattan to the Bronx Veterans Hospital carrying a $100 bill. When she reached her destination and wanted to pay the cab driver with this bill, he went crazy. Having all the insulation from life a university appointment confers, she proceeded to a local *bodega* (Puerto Rican grocery store) for change and was promptly laughed out of the store as Spanish expletives abounded. Finally, in desperation, she offered to take the cab driver to lunch so that she could get change to pay him. This was all he had to hear. "Vhat do I need a tin broad like you ven I have a vonderful vife vaiting for me in Brooklyn. I didn't come to de Bronx to get laid. I just vant my money. Dere is something wrong vit da air in de Bronx. Everyone's crazy."

As my partners escorted the professor to a local bank, I remained with the cab driver.

"I vant you should arrest her," he demanded.

"Now wait a minute," I replied, "You're going to get your money."

"But I'm vasting my time in dis crazy area. Arrest her!"

"Let me explain something to you. I'm not really a cop; I'm a police humanist working on a project in which I observe police behavior."

That did it—the cab driver almost keeled over. "D'er all crazy here. I must get back to Brooklyn. No vonder de Yankees are tinking about leaving de Bronx. Crazy. It's jus' crazy here." As soon as the professor returned from the bank, the cab driver drove away rapidly, searching for any highway out of "the crazy borough" as a throng of interested parties, *bodega* owners, bank employees, and one police-humanist laughed until the tears were streaming from their eyes.

Although the average police officer has tremendous leverage in making decisions on the street, he is hamstrung by borough command decisions. A hands-off attitude on illegal social clubs where whiskey, drugs, and guns are bought and sold is one such policy. It allows for criminal sanctuaries in every abandoned building in which an enterprising person has set up shop. The argument is made that the police cannot do everything—and of course they cannot—but the same activity that is crushed in Brooklyn is permitted in the Bronx. Policemen can go on for hours about criminal relativism—and with good reason.

It has also been brought to my attention that the city administration gave

$70 a week to members of the Ching-a-Lings (a youth gang) to escort elderly women to the supermarket. That in itself is no issue, except that this was an extortion payment to the very same gang that preyed on the elderly, and the money is used to buy weapons that are subsequently employed in a wide variety of criminal activities, including and especially armed robbery. Because the Ching-a-Lings are now engaged in a "city project," the police have been told to "lay off" gang members, and their headquarters in a renovated building has become as safe a criminal sanctuary as the medieval university.

When the police are not constrained by the political demands of superiors, they often face the condescension of those in interacting institutions. The assistant district attorneys, for example—who are upper-middle class, ritualistically liberal, possess an attitude of superiority that is cultivated in law school, and are embittered by the fact that they earn less than police officers—invariably have a patronizing attitude toward the police. When an arrest is made, the assistant district attorney starts his interrogation with the assumption the officer has no case. "Did you inform this fellow of his constitutional rights?" "Are you sure no provocation or entrapment was demonstrated in this arrest?" There is nothing wrong with these questions and I am glad they are asked, but the tone usually suggests the officer does not know what he is doing or, at the very least, has made an error in the arrest procedure.

At one hearing in Traffic Court, the arbiter in discussing a summons Kenny had dispensed, said, "Officer, are you sure you understand the rules of the road?" The question was dripping with condescension and Kenny blew up. It was hard for me to think of any other kind of response. After all, he spends eight hours of every day riding a squad car and enforcing the rules of the road. Why should the arbiter assume Kenny did not understand traffic laws?

These are minor irritants that, in the aggregate, create intense stress. It is amazing that the police generally maintain equilibrium on the job. Police work, more often than not, has constant tension and a lack of resolution. Jobs are not like television productions that have a beginning, middle, and end, with two pauses for a commercial break. Police activity is chaotic, seemingly lacking in purpose, and yet is indispensable. The police officer cannot make the Bronx a better place to live. He cannot stop the arson or stem the decay. He cannot find jobs and he cannot influence politicians. He is often a pawn trapped between civil libertarians and artificial production rates that measure his effectiveness. He is asked to put his finger in a dyke long after the flood is uncontrollable. He will remain unappreciated and his tasks are unavoidably Sisyphean.

My fantasies are gone. I no longer wish to be a police officer. In fact, even the empty platitudes of university life seem less offensive after this experience. However, there is a new-found and deeper appreciation for the thankless police job. I now have the belief that my life is a little better for having known two fine police officers, and I suspect that, when the elegy of the Bronx is written and, phoenix-like, this area rises from the ashes, some kind words will be said for those policemen who genuinely cared when so few cared about them.

April 1, 1978

62

The Minority on the Astor Place Station

I am a regular user of the New York subway system, a condition that puts me in the company of about a million people. I pick up a subway train at the IRT Astor Place station, a fact that puts me in the company of thousands of New Yorkers. And I am one of the few people who pays for the privilege of using the subway at this stop, a statement that reveals much about the majority of riders at this station.

The Astor Place station is an example of anarchy on display. To the left of the infrequently used toll booth is a fence about three feet high. At almost all hours of the day and night young men are seated on this fence poised to jump onto the platform. When a train approaches, a line up of people push the turnstile back so they can slip through the barrier without the insertion of a token. At Astor Place cheating the Metropolitan Transit Authority is a way of life.

Irritating as these cheaters are, they are trifling compared to the thief who routinely puts a slug in the slot so that your token cannot be inserted. With a deft motion of his sleek metal plunger he removes the slug and your token and, to add insult to injury, pulls the turnstile back so that you can slide around the barrier onto the station. This fellow dressed in a gray fedora and wine-colored sweater can be found selling these tokens he steals at 51st Street when commuters are frustrated by the rush hour line at the one toll booth on the uptown side.

So matter of fact is this petty and not so petty theft that the Astor Place toll booth employee rarely looks up from the rolls of dollars he is counting to observe the chaos around him. He is inured to the scene, since it can be observed every day of the week and every hour of the day a subway police-man isn't present. Of course, even when a cop is on the station the fence-sitter can be found waiting till the very last moment the train doors close before jumping the fence and entering a subway car. There isn't much any police officer can do.

What the scene at Astor Place represents is a city run amok. This form of relatively petty crime unravels the fabric of social order. Law-abiding people—I include myself here—wonder if we are the chumps. After all I can scale that three-foot barrier as easily as the youthful fence-sitters poised to beat the system. When a significant number of people maintains that the laws do not apply to them and have no fear of penalty or punishment for violating legal sanctions, the social norms that prevent a war of each against all are straining at the seams.

A talented guitarist plays progressive jazz riffs whose sound bounces from one wall to another in the corridor of the newly decorated Astor Place station. New York University students can be seen with books in hand chatting about a lecture in an introductory philosophy class. Several mothers wheel strollers onto the station, discussing the Sesame Street production they're taking the children to see in Madison Square Garden. Surrounding these people are the ubiquitous cheats, those without the slightest regard for the law.

Some people will regard my description as accurate but nonetheless an overreaction. These thieves are culpable of no more than stealing a one-way subway ride worth $1. It seems silly to get so exercised about this petty crime when more serious crimes are occurring all around us. Alas, this is true, but in some sense it is irrelevant. For what these cheats steal is not merely a ride, but the civic trust on which public institutions depend. Unless we become a police state, God forbid, some degree of inner restraint is needed to neutralize relative freedom. Without this internalized conscience, anarchy is in the offing or freedom is imperiled.

This Burkean formulation for social harmony has been lost on some New York youths who have grown up without the slightest understanding of civil behavior. They are the urban feral children preying on law-abiding citizens and mocking the laws of the body politic. Why should they pay for what can be taken without penalty? Where is the moral inhibition that restrains crimi-nality?

I stand on the Astor Place station virtually powerless to do anything about the cheaters in my midst. At the very least I'd like to wipe the self-satisfied smile off the faces of those who break the law with impunity. It was said by a cop in the film *Moscow on the Hudson* that New York is "a place where you can do anything." Certainly that claim has its positive side in our liberties and tolerance for eccentricity. But as I watch the cheats on Astor Place I wish there were a few restraints on license so that those who follow the laws don't feel as if they are a minority watching the columns of civil order collapse.

February 16, 1988

63

The Law in the Streets of East Harlem

A forty-one-year-old man was beaten to death by an angry crowd in Harlem after stealing $20 from a youthful woman. Neighborhood residents watching the chase shouted words of encouragement to the attackers. So inured to street crime are these residents that it was described by many observers as "another average day in East Harlem."

Yet there is another side to this story. It is the fact that this act of wanton brutality was not a major news story. Other acts of brutality such as the two British officers slain at the hands of an Irish mob or the Israeli soldier killed while on duty in Bethlehem have relegated this grisly local tale to the back pages of the newspaper.

In one respect this is unusual: local events usually get more attention than international issues. The reason it didn't happen in this case is because robbery and brutality are a predictable part of the city's landscape. People don't shock anymore.

Ann Beteran, aged twenty-one, was at the bakery counter with a $20 bill in her hand when Raymondo Carraballo, a known drug addict, snatched the money and ran from the store. Beteran ran after Carraballo shouting to a crowd of passersby. The crowd soon became a mob, chasing the thief until he was trapped and then pummeled him with sticks, fists, and a garbage-can cover. Carraballo died several hours later at Mount Sinai Hospital.

One resident of the neighborhood said, "He was probably a crackhead and didn't even know what he was doing." Another argued, "It could have been someone's mother who was robbed." Of course, both claims may be true.

What is unquestionably true is the breakdown of state authority. In places like Harlem, with drug trafficking an open enterprise, citizen resentment is institutionalized. Residents know there isn't a police-enforcement system; there is only the law in the streets. An arrest is correlated to a release. Rikers Island prison can hold only so many assailants. And neighborhoods like Harlem are assailant farms.

The people who saw this murder firsthand reacted in the way you would expect anyone to respond who has been brutalized by crack dealers and users and lives with the fear that someone with a gun may take his hard-earned money or his life. Resentment on the streets is at a fever pitch. The cops at the Twenty-fifth Precinct in East Harlem aren't to blame. They do the best they can under conditions that worsen each day. But they, like everyone else in that community, know the odds aren't on their side.

The criminals learned that lesson some time ago. When punishment is milder than the severity of the crime, it is only a matter of time before young thugs realize there is little to lose and much to gain from the life of dealing. Drug dealers are now recruited at thirteen so that if they are apprehended they can only be treated as youthful offenders. That translates into a slap on the wrist and an unintended legal wink suggesting that you can return to the world of crime. One of the wealthiest men in Harlem is the Peugot bicycle dealer. Teenagers aren't old enough to buy Cadillacs.

Is it any wonder that retribution is so close to the surface? Young men and women with needle tracks on their arms are on a daily search for the score, the money that buys them a new high. Every law-abiding, income-earning member of the community realizes he is a potential next target. There is no neutral zone in Harlem. There is no way to declare yourself a noncombatant.

There certainly aren't enough prison cells for all the thugs. There aren't enough tough judges in this town. There aren't enough cops on the street. And there isn't enough supervision and concern in the home. The blame can't all be leveled at the authorities. When one realizes that the crucible of hate has reached the boiling point, it is not surprising that neighborhood residents would turn into an angry, murderous mob. They have had enough and can't take it anymore.

That a robbery should turn into a street murder and that this event should be treated as merely another of many gruesome events indicates how far down the slippery slope of barbarism we have traveled. No matter how lurid this story may be, tomorrow's headlines will be worse. For the residents of East Harlem there is almost nothing that can shock them any longer.

June 3, 1988

64

Our Streets: A Cafeteria
of Uncontrolled Substances

"East side, west side, all around the town . . ." goes the refrain to an old tune that can now be updated to reveal a theme much less innocent than the light fantastic tripped by me and Mamie O'Rourke on the sidewalks of New York. From the East Side to the West and the uptown to down, a city stroller can now observe the open and blatant sale of hard drugs.

In fact, walking the streets of New York is like observing an open-air drug bazaar. The dealing isn't restricted to one location, like Harlem, nor are the transactions conducted in secrecy. In New York it is easier to get hashish than in Marrakech. One can buy coke in midtown streets almost as easily as Jordache tops from a vendor in front of Saks Fifth Avenue. And marijuana is as accessible as Kent cigarets, although it is not yet in vending machines.

On Park Avenue and 52nd Street in front of the Fuji Bank, drug vendors begin dealing at 11:30 A.M. and quit about 2:00 P.M. to accommodate the lunch crowd that wants some smoke or a snort or two. Construction workers as well as young executives in three-piece suits stand on line waiting patiently for their turn. It is interesting that the vendors carry attaché cases like their executive counterparts. Since they deal in cash exclusively, providing change is a requisite for their business activity.

In Washington Square Park, barkers can be heard at all hours of the day shouting: "I've got David Kennedy coke, the finest stuff money can buy. I'll take cash, checks, or Master Charge." Jean-clad, acne-skinned youths parade through the park buying drugs the way my parents used to examine wares in Orchard Street pushcarts. What is startling is that everyone is approached; men in business suits, kids just entering puberty, instructors at New York University, even old women from a generation when snow came from the sky and horses left manure, not needle marks.

Fifth Avenue and 42nd Street is still one of the most glamorous corners in the world, but is has a new influence, the library hawkers. This breed of salesmen deals in drugs exclusively. They sit on the steps or walk along the path to Bryant Park. It is no coincidence that purse snatchers can be found stationed right on the corner: two youths between fifteen and seventeen wearing ski parkas, jeans, and sneakers. One jostles a woman, while the other grabs her bag. In five minutes they can be found in Bryant Park buying heroin. It is their life cycle: theft, drugs, the high, and then starting all over again.

At Morningside Park and 116th Street in the shadow of Columbia University, drugs are employed as a medium of financial transactions. As much as an ounce of coke is used as a bet on a given game, the winning team getting the coke as its reward for victory. A postgame party means getting higher on coke than one normally gets jumping at the basket.

What is unusual about this description is that it is no longer considered unusual. With liberalized drug laws supported by the Carey administration, with the police incapable of addressing all activity on the streets, with public complacency, with courts filled to overflowing with violent crimes, street drug sales are simply another familiar feature of city life.

Perhaps the strain of urban living makes drug consumption irresistible. Perhaps we are evolving into a new mode of life, one that tolerates an acceptance of hard drugs. Perhaps the permissive climate has not yet determined appropriate limits for aberrational behavior.

As an observer of this drug scene, there is no acceptable explanation. The products of drug abuse appear as zombies in midtown doorways. They engage in crime that makes any self-respecting citizen wonder about walking the streets alone. The corrosive influence of hard drugs can immediately be felt in the vacant stares of once active and vibrant teenagers. For those who care about this city, this drug-distribution system on the streets deserves careful scrutiny. Otherwise, New York may decline very low from its ubiquitous high on the streets.

January 22, 1980

65

Professors, Clean Up Your Own Front Yards

It often is argued that with all of the university talent available in New York there should be a ready supply of ideas for eliminating city problems. Presumably the advocates of using this brain trust believe that the scholarly pursuits of university professors can be employed to improve urban conditions.

However, those who take this position usually know very little about scholars. They also are myopic about the community where scholars hang their hats. Take as an illustration the three most prestigious universities in New York and the communities where these institutions are located. The one striking fact is, that New York University, Columbia, and the City University Graduate Center are adjacent to parks—Washington Square, Morningside, and Bryant, respectively.

Those parks are supposed to provide refuge from the tedium of research, a respite from boring classes. They are the enclave for those weary of cement and crowds. That is, of course, the theory. As anyone who has been to these parks can tell you, they are dominated by drug peddlers. They are as safe as the former demilitarized zone in Vietnam and are the refuge for society's detritus. They are the crime zones. If the naïve or unwary should find their way into their paths at night, there is no telling their fate.

Yet the interesting point is that the shadow of each of the universities mentioned is cast onto a park. Professors may spend twenty-five years of their professional lives peering out of office windows to the appalling park scene down below.

Every one of them is familiar with the conditions. It is not as if there is a disagreement over this description. Each and every faculty has devoted time to the problem. But there is not the slightest bit of evidence that our parks are safe for the average person who simply wants to rest under a shaded tree.

If evidence ever were needed to demonstrate professorial impotence, here it is. It should be noted that this inability to improve conditions in one's backyard has not inhibited these same faculty members from proposing policy on South Africa, federal assistance to students, or defense expenditures.

It rarely has occurred to anyone that you should resist giving advice until you put your own house in order. The signs of anomie that the university scholars discuss in Emile Durkheim's works are found in abundance in our parks. The evidence of anarchy that Edmund Burke so eloquently described when inner controls over behavior are not manifest is reinforced by the thugs who rule the parks.

The silliness of the Rousseauian belief that indigenes have the inner resources to educate themselves is made palpable by the park environment. Nonetheless, books and ideas are kept separate from life. When a professor is beaten into submission or mugged or even killed, there will be a moment when the faculty is mobilized. But then normalcy returns as do the bums and thugs.

One weaves in and out of the park like a ball carrier trying to avoid his pursuers. The congnoscenti do not sit in the parks unless they are looking for trouble or drugs. Permissiveness is the reigning view at our universities. To challenge it one must take on one's colleagues, the ACLU, the city administration, and the judicial system. It simply isn't worth it. After all, the parks in question seem to exist as a justification for the Second Law of Thermodynamics.

The scholars throw up their hands in despair. The administrations say that "things are getting better," albeit everyone knows that this institutional lie is for the benefit of parents and prospective faculty recruits.

The answer to the problem, the only answer our eminent faculty types can come up with, is to stay out. Proclamations are made from on high that you enter these parks at your own risk. This is the scholarly answer: We can't protect you. We can't devise a way to defend you. And we can't retrieve from the thugs what is rightfully not theirs.

Is it any wonder students are skeptical about scholarly contributions to the social order? Is it all surprising that many people in this nation do not believe academics can solve problems? Was it unusual for Thorstein Veblen to describe scholars as those trained in incapacity?

The signs are clear. Our universities are growing in size. Our faculties win plaudits. Our faculty members receive honors. But the parks across the street from ivy-covered buildings are rotten with a cancer that metastasized in full public view. It is an open admission that our universities have no answers and their scholars are impotent.

April 25, 1985

66

Washington Square Park Redux

If one is curious to know what the city might be like if the sensibilities of civil libertarians ruled the cultural roost, one need not look any further than Washington Square Park. In this once beautiful little park that prompted the musings of Henry James, Edith Wharton, John Dos Passos, Thomas Wolfe, among others, drug dealers conduct their nefarious trade with impunity. This park that stands as one of the city's most enduring landmarks is acknowledged by politician and police officer to have been converted into a drug bazaar that seemingly defies solution.

Drug dealers have made the park their turf. They have literally forced the kids out of the playground and have discouraged the elderly—who used to sing songs from the '20s and '30s to the accompaniment of an accordionist—from the east side of the park. The park has surrendered to drug dealers.

If the police arrest someone, the person is very often back in the park before the cop is back on his beat. If the drug dealer is sentenced to prison, it is usually for a two-week stint, what dealers call their "overhead." While there are residents of the community appalled by conditions in the park, there are influential members of the community who consider any effort to restrict access to be a violation of civil liberties. At one meeting the suggestion that a fence be built around Washington Square Park with one entrance and exit was greeted with jeers. "What do you want to do, build the Berlin Wall in Greenwich Village?" asked a long-time community resident.

An exceptionally tall, about six-foot, nine-inch, black dealer stations himself on the east side of the park. He takes orders from passing cars and calls a phone booth on Washington Place on the west side. As the car circles the park the drug transaction is made by his colleague in crime. The driver doesn't even stop to make his "score." It is done as matter-of-factly as buying hamburgers at the drive-in.

These conditions have been observed for years. The cops watch in resignation. When a resident of the community blows his top, he is often told by the

149

thugs to leave the park if he doesn't want to get hurt. After all, the park belongs to "them." Each spring there is a rally in the park for the legalization of marijuana. Opposing points of view aren't entertained. The history of liberalism in Greenwich Village fosters permissiveness. "Everything goes in Washington Square Park" a neighbor of mine said proudly. Alas, that is true.

Most students and faculty members at New York University walk through the park with mental blinders. The words "smokes, smokes" and "smack for sale" are part of the environment, like the air one breathes. In fact the crack smoke is in the air one breathes. Each day in front of the Garibaldi statue the drug dealers convene. Recently I overheard one say, "The undercover guys are going off duty." There isn't a drug dealer who can't identify the under-cover cops, who doesn't know his legal rights, and who carries more than the legal limit of dope for a felony offense.

When you talk to any persons about Washington Square Park, they throw up their hands in despair. The response is understandable because the liberal psychology is conventional wisdom. But let's say, for example, a wall were constructed around the park with one cop at the entrance. Let's say, for the sake of argument, that anyone arrested for drugs got a mandatory sentence. It seems to me plea bargaining for drug dealers shouldn't be permitted. Let's say the park were reclaimed by decent people and the cops forbade anyone from entering the park who had been arrested for drug sales.

I'm not sure these recommendations would perform miracles. But I am sure they would have a salutary effect on the present anarchistic conditions. I also suspect there are supporters of my position in the community. After all, the mayor lives only one block from the park. But in the last analysis what is right and sensible to do is not what will be done. It's not that we can't cope with the drug problem, it's that few people are willing to pay the price for the solution.

January 31, 1987

67

It Isn't Drugs That He's Pushing

He walks down the street with a swagger that suggests arrogance. The big white hat with a plume gently sways in the breeze; the three-piece white suit fits like a glove; the colorful handkerchief drapes from his jacket pocket; the high-heeled shoes that tap out music as they hit the sidewalk are symbols of a dude on the make. To complete the image—one that has been so carefully arranged—there is a car. Not just any car, but a cream-colored Continental that is sleek, fast, and an eye-catcher. The man has style; it is the style of the Harlem streets. When you have it, you flaunt it because it gives you instant influence.

This man pushes no drugs, he isn't a pimp, and he has never been arrested. He is honest, deeply religious, and sensitive. Although few people know it, he is an undercover cop.

For him the culture of the streets is natural. He was born and lives in the ghetto. He knows jive talk and he can still hit a jump shot from twenty feet. He is, incidentally, among the most effective cops in the department at tracking down drug distributors. His arrest record is like a *Who's Who* of the Harlem "Mafia." I'll call him Johnny.

Yet, despite the success, the commendations, citations, and shields, it is becoming increasingly difficult for him to do his job. It may seem odd but the biggest obstacle in the way of his task is the law-enforcement administration to which he reports.

The jurisdictional struggle that takes place between the New York Police Department, the New York Drug Enforcement Task Force, the Federal Drug Enforcement Administration, United States Customs, and other law-enforcement agencies often interferes with arrests even when the evidence of wrongdoing is undeniable. The Drug Enforcement Administration has regional authority over drug abuse as a function of its Justice Department affiliation. Its ostensible mission is to apprehend the big dealers. However, its staff, composed of officials from all over the country, simply does not possess the expertise to cope with the well-developed drug distribution system in this city. A guy from New Mexico, no matter how intelligent, can't possibly understand the street scene the way Johnny does. Yet the Drug Enforcement Administration uses its jurisdictional authority to subordinate other agencies, at times even undermining local police investigations into drug dealing.

Recently, Johnny was working with a former dealer who turned informant; the dealer wanted to get a reduced sentence and another identity. The case forced Johnny to go south where large drug transactions were taking place. When officials in the Drug Enforcement Administration learned of his trip, they maintained that a New York cop had no jurisdiction in that area. At this point, they insisted on full control over the investigation. But their manner was so heavy-handed that the informant feared leaks and refused to cooperate. The "Southern connection" with an alleged $2 million-a-week handle is still in business and the case is in limbo.

The investigation of Leroy "Nicky" Barnes, once considered the biggest heroin dealer in New York City before he received a life-imprisonment sentence in 1978, went back to Task Force surveillance in 1972. But the Drug Enforcement Administration took full credit for his conviction in 1977, even though it had no early contact with the issue. In fact, if it had not been for the extension of the federal conspiracy laws that allow a liberal interpretation of conspiracy, the Drug Enforcement Administration would never have been involved in the case at all. In this matter, as in so many other cases, Johnny, who was making buys from Nicky Barnes in an effort to accumulate evidence, and the New York Drug Enforcement Task Force got none of the credit for the arrest.

With the drug problem quickly becoming a social plague, with teenagers earning $500 a day as drug runners, and with more Mercedes-Benzes on Harlem streets than in many Westchester suburbs, imagining New York City as drug capital of the world is not farfetched. Clearly, these kids making $500 a day aren't going to take a job washing dishes when they are twenty years old. Basketball games on 116th Street and Morningside Park are now played for $1,000 a game. It will obviously be a lot more difficult to contain the drug problem in the future, if for no other reason than the coming to adulthood of the drug-running adolescents.

Where does that leave the Johnnys of this town? Frustrated on the job. Johnny believes in his mission. He wants to clean up the streets but wonders if the bureaucratic mess will permit it. He wants to turn black teenagers' minds around but has only his belief in God to offer. When the runners see his threads they admire him. But his real message can't be seen. Like a character out of one of Stendhal's novels, the public person makes compromises so that his private beliefs may remain intact.

The Police Department is lucky to have Johnny even if it doesn't know it. It would really be something if the brass let him do his job, perhaps rewarded him for a job well done. In the last analysis, Johnny is a Sisyphus masquerading as a public servant. But he is still the best action in town.

April 21, 1979

68

Extending Judicial Power

It is often said by defenders of activist courts that decisions rendered by judges with this disposition do not have a deleterious influence on the society and very often have positive social results. More often than not it is hard to determine the veracity of this claim. After all, measuring the social effect of a court decision is virtually impossible. However, a recent decision in New York demonstrates with extraordinary clarity what potential damage can be done when a judge with an activist sensibility stretches the limits of legal precedent.

Judge Lewis L. Douglass, who sits on the State Supreme Court in Brooklyn, ordered a convicted heroin dealer to pay more than $2 million in restitution. It was argued that the money should be used to support drug rehabilitation programs in New York City. The sum of money was determined by estimating the number of addicts the seized heroin would addict and multiplying that number by the cost of rehabilitation for each addict.

While I am firmly behind ''throwing the book'' at drug dealers and believe that ''blood money'' should revert to the state, there are several aspects of this decision that cry out for commentary because they go beyond legal precedent. In his order Justice Douglass said that in most criminal cases involving restitution ''the court will know the specific victim and how much he or she lost.'' This is not so in drug cases, the judge said, even though ''it is beyond debate that drug dealers create victims.''

These arguments, which on the face of it appear unexceptional, are laden with legal baggage. The idea that a formula exists for restitution smacks of social-science theory on which so much of court-enhanced power is based. But in what sense is social science a depiction of the way the world works? If a physician takes Demerol but manages to conduct his professional life well, does he owe his patients restitution for the improved care they might have received if he did not use drugs? If a baseball player's batting average declines because of the use of drugs, does he owe restitution to owners and fans for the level of play they had come to expect from him before drug use affected his performance? Clearly, social science in the service of judicial power ends up as no better than superstition.

Second, the idea that it is "indisputable" that drug dealers create victims is not only disputable, it defies logic. A drug dealer doesn't create a drug user, unless of course one assumes that free will doesn't exist. In suggesting this immutable link between dealer and user, the judge like so many of his colleagues, was ignoring the argument for individual responsibility. Ultimately everyone is responsible for his actions, notwithstanding the always available temptations in our midst. Drug dealing is against the law and should be punished as a violation of that law. It does not follow that a drug dealer creates users. If anything, users create dealers.

The pathology of drug abuse is a matter of self-inflicted harm. A user wants to hurt himself. The dealer makes the drug available, but he doesn't produce the harm. This distinction appears to be overlooked by Judge Douglass and for a perfectly obvious reason. Many courts have arrived at the conclusion that responsibility for illicit acts belongs with the society, not the individual. The attribution of cause is exogenous. People take drugs because they are out of work, anxious about social dislocation, dismayed with the state of the world. Rarely will this judicial school concede that many people take drugs because they want to take them. That, in effect, they have made a decision to harm themselves and often others.

That sense of personal responsibility is built into a constitutional order that relies on "we the people" not "we the state" or "we the society." "We" is a collectivity of individual atoms each sovereign over some aspect of their lives. That sovereignty exercised in the use of drugs should be seen against the backdrop of civic order and the maintenance of law.

It seems to me drug dealers should be prosecuted to the full extent of the law; users who take drugs illicitly should be prosecuted to the full extent of the law. But it makes no sense to confuse personal responsibility with collective guilt, unless, of course, judicial decisions are unrelated to legal precedent and are designed to extend judicial authority.

April 14, 1988

69

What Happens When "Vagrants" Become "Homeless"

It is something of a bromide to contend that ideas have consequences or that words are ideas incarnate. But at no time have these bromides been more poignant than at this very moment. For several years we have been told about a new class of people called "the homeless." As the word might suggest, these are presumably people without homes. Some of the homeless do indeed fall into this category of not having a place to live. But this in no way describes these people. Moreover, by employing the word "homeless" instead of the word "vagrant," which has gone out of fashion, the issue has been transmogrified from a social to a housing problem.

Ignored in the new designation is what many people always knew about vagrants: many of them are criminals. However, the word "homeless" has concealed the existence of this element. In order to find a place for those wandering the streets during the bitterly cold winter months, Grand Central Terminal is used as a refuge, a welcome refuge, for the so-called homeless.

But in a recent television program derived from Metro North Police Chief John Esposito's report, the homeless population is said to include individuals with extensive records of theft and violent crime. Most of the crimes are committed by the homeless against the homeless. At the terminal, assaults increased in one year by 233 percent, robberies rose by 196 percent, burglaries were up by 85 percent. While the report contends commuters are rarely affected—a point I regard as rather dubious—shopkeepers in the terminal are often the targets of crime.

It is hard to believe that in the nation's busiest rail terminal, criminals, prostitutes, victims, and the insane rub shoulders literally and figuratively with some of New York's most prominent business figures commuting from Westchester and Putnam counties. Most of these commuters walk quickly with their heads down; they make a point of avoiding eye contact with the homeless.

One day as I was walking from the main terminal to the entrance to the IRT subway, a young homeless man wielding a straight-edged razor wished to engage me in conversation. I didn't slow down to find out what he wanted. Fortunately, I didn't end up a crime statistic, but that's primarily because I put on my psychological blinders and put my legs into overdrive.

Predictably, spokespeople for the homeless contend that Grand Central is not a good place for anyone to live. Of course, this is true, but beside the point. Most of these spokespeople express surprise at the rise in crime attributed to the homeless. But the only reason this could be surprising is that these unthinking supporters have not recognized the criminals who represent a portion of the homeless population. The cliché applied to these vagrants in the terminal is that they are pitiful creatures who "wouldn't harm a fly." Now we learn that the fly has been pinned and its wings torn off.

Police officials contend that unless the force is beefed up considerably, they will lose the war against crime. This statement is also beside the point. The fact is Grand Central Terminal should not have been converted into a shelter for the homeless. In what sense is it an expression of compassion to allow the criminal element to assault other homeless people, to bring terror to proprietors, and to brutalize the atmosphere in one of New York's architectural wonders? Those who are down on their luck belong in shelters; those who are mentally incompetent belong in hospitals; those who are criminals belong in jail.

Before the term "homeless" was in vogue, it was easy to make these distinctions. Unfortunately, a change in phraseology has affected our thinking. In my opinion what we require, even more than institutional change, is clarity of language. These people on our streets are vagrants. As was always the case, some in that group are criminals. It is absurd to tar all these people with the same brush and it is inhumane to ignore their plight. But one can't begin to do something about this issue until the vocabulary employed in stating the problem reveals what is going on.

May 28, 1987

70

Is the Howard Beach Incident
a Racial Issue?

Like a hair trigger poised to fire, the proponents of racial explanations have let loose a fusillade of bigotry in response to the hateful assault of three blacks by several teenagers in Howard Beach, Queens. Before the evidence was assembled, Mayor Koch called this "the most violent crime in New York's recent history." He then called for undercover police in Howard Beach to prevent such actions from recurring. And he followed this contentious remark with a call for a national commission to study racism.

If this didn't stir the brew of racial antipathy, there were Reverends Sharpton, Daughtry, and West who claim that a black man cannot obtain justice in this city. Alton Maddox, the lawyer for one of the black victims, charged that the driver of the car that struck and killed Michael Griffith was a willing participant in the assault—even though there did not appear to be a shred of evidence to support this claim.

Charges and countercharges have made this incident into a racial conflict, albeit there are many unanswered questions in this case. Although Griffith was described as a "construction worker," he was shot in the chest in 1982 in a dispute with a suspected car thief with whom he was allegedly stealing cars. He was also a prime suspect in the slaying of a Brooklyn man who was gunned down "over a cigaret." When Griffith was struck and killed, a toy gun resembling a .32 revolver and a beeper were found near the body.

Timothy Grimes, another of the men attacked in Howard Beach, was arrested and charged with stabbing the woman with whom he lives. Sandiford, the third person attacked in the incident, also has an arrest record.

In the first report of the beatings the three black victims were said to have walked three miles up Cross Bay Boulevard in search of help for their disabled car. Later it was noted that they were on their way to the subway

159

station so they could get home. The contradictory accounts about what these men were doing in Howard Beach have not been resolved.

Nonetheless, whatever the circumstances for their presence in Howard Beach doesn't justify either the wanton beating of these men or a vigilante attack of possible hoods up to no good. However, if these men were up to no good, the exaggerated rhetoric about a racist attack is unwarranted. Yet the politicians, reporters, holy men, and lawyers who make a living crying "white racism" leaped at the opportunity to use this case for their own purposes. They finally had an example to cite. And cite it they did.

Before the evidence was in, before a trial was held, before the eyewitnesses had testified, before an explanation was offered for the reluctance of a victim to testify, the answers were proferred fully digested. Racism was the consensus culprit. That many Howard Beach residents deplored the attack was ignored in the media hype. The *New York Times* reported that the assault "is widely perceived as the worst racial incident in New York City in years." But who is it that perceives the assault in this way? Was the rape and murder of a talented white actress on a rooftop by a black assailant not a racial attack? What makes it less violent than the assault and later death of Griffith? Is the rape and murder of a white eighty-one-year-old by a teenage black assailant in Brooklyn not a racist attack?

What most blacks and whites in this city share is a loathing of crime. Since blacks are the victims in a disproportionate number of crimes, they can fully appreciate the fact that crime doesn't distinguish between races. The attempts made to cast the Howard Beach assault as an example of racism that bubbled to the surface ignores the complexity and idiosyncratic character of this crime. It seems that a group of thugs acting out of vigilante justice or plain hate beat three blacks "on their turf."

No sensible person can justify this behavior. But it is also true that sensible people should not rank crimes, should not offer explanations of motives before the evidence is available, and should not use such incidents for their own self-aggrandizement. Racism isn't rampant in Howard Beach or New York City. This was a terrible crime. Any survivor of violent crime will tell you all violent crime is terrible. But before general comments are made about New York City and this society based on the incident in Queens, it behooves the media analysts to seach for light instead of thunder in Howard Beach.

January 22, 1987

71

Reclaiming New York's Prisons
from the Inmates

Controller Harrison Goldin's recent audit indicates that the commissaries at City jails sold contraband—such as knives, smoking pipes, and other paraphernalia for drug use—to inmates. While jails' supply boss Edward Lepkowski is at the center of a wide-ranging probe, there is a dimension to this scandal that demands further investigation.

At places like Rikers Island the inmates run the prison. Guards are there to keep prisoners from escaping. But the actual operation of these facilities is for all practical purposes under the control of the inmates. It is not at all coincidental that the colors of local gangs fly from the rooftop of Rikers. The symbol of sovereignty in this nation is replaced on this prison site by the flag of thugs. If ever imagery told a story, here it is.

Why then should it be surprising that contraband goods are sold to the prisoners? Within the walls inmates make the rules. If might makes right—the prevailing legal principle at most New York jails—then one joins a gang to survive. If theft is not penalized but leads to rewards, the behavior is bound to be reinforced in jail. It is not coincidental that at the Brooklyn House of Detention $10,500 worth of inmate belongings are unaccounted for this year.

It is obviously something of a charade to argue that prisoners can be rehabilitated. In New York prisons, antisocial behavior is the only way to survive. What one learns behind prison walls serves to make released inmates a menace on the streets. That is the reality either ignored or not faced up to by city administrators.

In order to do something about this issue the administration would be obliged to tackle some knotty problems. For one thing, additional guards would have to be hired so that the frightening ratio of prisoners to guards can be reversed. A July 4 attack of Rikers Island inmates on several guards is only the latest incident in a jail with a history of violent attacks.

It is also the case that prisons are overcrowded. New facilities are desperately needed. Whether that means renovating old ferries into prison facilities or constructing modular correction facilities, something has to be done and municipal funds will have to be spent.

Last, and perhaps most important, prisons have to be retaken from the inmates. While this seems like a rather bizarre idea, it isn't. Anyone who has been obliged to spend time in a city facility knows the terror of being an "unaffiliated" prisoner. It is the equivalent of being hunted without a means of protection. This is also the most inflammatory recommendation.

Since the genuine prison leaders are found in the ranks of the inmates, this reform can unsettle the well-established prison norms leading to consequences with devastating effect. Stability—to the extent it exists—is created and enforced by prison leaders. They make the rules; neither the courts nor law-enforcement agents actually determine the behavior behind cell blocks.

If there is a compelling reason for reform at this juncture it is not to be found in Goldin's audit, but in the spread of AIDS, particularly in a prison population with a disproportionate number of "high-risk groups," homosexuals and intravenous drug users. The prisoner sentenced to a six-month term who is raped at a New York detention center may end up with a premature death sentence. If the authorities cannot control the prison population, the scourge of AIDS may wipe it out.

The Goldin audit certainly illustrates the rampant illegality in our prisons. But it is barely the tip of the proverbial iceberg. Inmate control behind the walls of New York's detention centers is a corrosive influence on criminal justice and represents a life-threatening prospect for anyone who ends up in a municipal jail. Whether New York officials are willing to tackle this problem or not, the spread of AIDS will soon make it unavoidable.

July 28, 1987

72

Polishing One of the Apple's Public Pools

Several weeks ago I wrote a piece entitled "Polishing the Apple" for the *New York Post*. It was an attempt to describe modest efforts at reclaiming some of New York's institutions from decay and barbarism. The response was overwhelming.

Perhaps the most touching letters came from a group of sixth-graders in Bedford-Stuyvesant at P.S. 305. These students contend that if I can "improve conditions" in other institutions perhaps I can help them "reclaim" a public swimming pool in their neighborhood.

They allege that the pool is "infested" with drug dealers. These kids claim their valuables are taken from the lockers. They contend the older kids beat them up. It is argued that broken glass and trash are thrown into the pool.

I was touched by the poignancy of these notes; I was also flattered that these youngsters might reach out to me believing, as they seemingly do, that my articles can affect conditions in their neighborhood. On the other hand, these letters raise questions about mediating services, for example, the Police Department and the Parks Department and the borough president's office, of which they might avail themselves.

I decided to investigate. The pool is located on Marcy Avenue across the street from a junior high school. While the pool is officially called the Kosciusko Pool, everyone I talked to referred to it simply as the "Marcy Pool."

It is a large pool with graffiti on every wall. Radio parts litter the sides of the pool. Bricks have been thrown into the pool itself. The clock on the deep end is in disrepair. In fairness to Parks Department personnel, clean-up of the area isn't scheduled to begin until the end of May and the opening isn't scheduled until June.

The community relations officers in the local Seventy-ninth Precinct are aware of the problems. During the summer months five cops are assigned to

163

the pool on a regular basis. One burly officer, assigned to the front gate, maintains that the lockers are routinely rifled. He admonishes kids to keep personal belongings with them.

My assessment is that the police and park attendants are doing about as well as their resources will permit. With 1,000 people at the pool on a hot summer day, it is impossible to monitor every fight and every minor infraction of the law.

However, the letter-writing children do raise valid issues. It would make sense to have an attendant in the locker rooms to discourage theft. In fact, it probably makes sense to hire several dozen neighborhood adolescents to be pool monitors. One can't expect five cops to deal with every issue that might arise when 1,000 youngsters get together to frolic in the sun. Since the city has a work program for youngsters in the summer months, several dozen should be assigned to the Marcy Pool.

That these students should have written to me is in some sense rather sad, since they didn't know where else to turn. Their frustration is understandable. After receiving the letters I decided to call the borough president's office. Since the borough president was away in Israel, I was referred to his aide. I called her fourteen times and on each occasion she was at a meeting. All I could think of was the exasperation of a sixth-grader trying to track her down.

In this era of cynicism, it is easy to believe that no one cares about the problems of others and that writing letters won't make a difference. I'd like the students in Kay Valdner's sixth-grade class to know that their letters inspired this article and I hope the attention given their neighborhood pool makes a difference.

But most important, I want these kids to believe that their letter writing is an exercise in democratic participation. They have the right to express themselves and the responsibility to be active members of their community. On both counts these youngsters have seemingly succeeded. Marcy Pool conditions may not improve overnight. But if they don't, these students should write another battery of letters till they do. Let me assure them that one class, one group of dedicated students, one conscientious teacher can make a difference in the life of this city and in their neighborhood.

April 30, 1987

73

A New Look at the Goetz Case

Recent revelations in the Goetz case may be changing public perceptions. If it is true that Bernhard Goetz fired at one of his accosters after he was helpless, it is argued, how can Goetz possibly discuss self-defense as his motive?

Sidney Schanberg, writing in the *New York Times* argues that "As a result of these facts emerging into public view, the mood has changed." Perhaps Schanberg is right. But there are some observations about this case that haven't been made, and are worth making.

The outpouring of initial support for Goetz demonstrates how fed up the public is with violent crime on the subways. Goetz may indeed be "a flake"—to use Mayor Koch's expression—but that doesn't mean he wouldn't feel the sense of terror and degradation that accompanies a mugging. Although the facts in this case haven't been ascertained, it is hard to look at the arrest record of the accosters and believe attorney William Kunstler's view that they were "panhandling." Panhandlers ask for money, they don't demand it.

Let us say, for the sake of argument, that the violence Goetz employed to defend himself was gratuitous. Can we lose sight of the fact that he was defending himself? After all, Goetz was beaten and robbed before; he didn't learn about crime by reading Schanberg's column in the *Times*. Moreover, what cannot be ignored in this case and in many such crimes is the gratuitous pain and anguish the victim may suffer. It is not only money that is taken but pride and self-respect.

One victim of a mugging said, "I don't remember how much money was taken from me. But there is one thing I will never forget. That thug with a gun in his hand forced me to get on my knees and call him 'sir.' That I will never forget."

For two weeks after the Goetz incident, subway crime declined by 40 percent. Although there may not be a direct causal relationship, it is ludicrous to ignore Goetz's effect on the criminal population. Wittingly or unwittingly, it was served notice. Every self-respecting rider of the subways secretly rejoiced in the shootings.

Now we are told that those who hyped Goetz as a hero are in retreat. Whatever this case actually shows, it cannot erase the ubiquity of crime in the subways. Bernhard Goetz may not be the most appropriate symbol of law and order. Nonetheless, he responded for everyone who is intimidated by the thugs who roam the underground passages of this city.

Perhaps the Goetz response to the actions of his accosters was not entirely warranted—a point that has not yet been determined. Nonetheless, who can sit in judgment of someone who resists a shakedown? I'm sure that Schanberg isn't a regular commuter on the subway. I'm equally sure that Kunstler hasn't been mugged.

For New Yorkers who are obliged to ride the trains and for those who have had the misfortune to be mugged, they will not retreat from defending Bernhard Goetz. He may not be all that we might like in a defender of law and order, but then again there are very few New Yorkers who have not been cowed by the street thugs and revolving-door justice.

If the Goetz case is turned into a media circus in which Goetz himself is deemed the offender, street crime will have won a victory in this city.

March 7, 1985

74

Liberals Put Fuel on Fire of City Crime

William Kunstler and the apostles of morality on the lunatic left contend that Bernhard Goetz, the so-called "subway vigilante" is a racist. After all, he is a white slayer of black youths. That in itself is sufficient to justify their charge. What, however, do these same self-appointed judges say when the "vigilante" is a working-class father of two, who is an ex-Marine and happens to be black?

On Thursday, February 21, Andy Frederick went to work as usual on the BMT subway line, except that this was to be a voyage unlike any other. In the bowels of the New York underground, Frederick observed two youths who were allegedly making fun of stealing candy from a vendor at the Broadway-Nassau Street station.

"Leave him alone . . . ," Frederick said. This response was what one would expect from any self-respecting citizen who hasn't been made cowardly by the rampant barbarism on the streets. Instead of simply walking away, the youths attacked Frederick, striking him on the side of the head with a beer bottle. In self-defense he pulled a two-inch pocket knife and stabbed one of his assailants in the chest. The young many died instantly.

Frederick purports to lead a clean life. The record bears this out. He has never committed a crime. He is a decent father and husband. He pays taxes. Nothing in his past suggests he would commit murder. There isn't a scintilla of evidence that he is a vigilante looking for crime so that he can arrogate to himself the roles of judge and jury. Frederick was simply put in the straitjacket of destiny.

The social dynamite waiting to explode on the streets and in the subways of the city is violent crime, committed ostensibly by black youths between the ages of fifteen and twenty-five. That is a statement of fact. As Frederick himself noted, "There are people out there—black, white, it doesn't matter." What does matter is that law-abiding citizens are hostages of fear.

For a considerable period our jurists have created the illusion that society can tolerate a different standard of behavior from black youths. In appearing to be sensitive to the plight of blacks, a racist double standard has been developed. That is why the thugs can rely on the Kunstlers of this world for legal assistance and even countersuits, while Andy Frederick fears for his future.

Other witnesses were on that Broadway-Nassau Street station. They might have assisted the vendor. But they "knew better." They've learned not to get involved. These thugs kill; it is not a Judeo-Christian conscience that serves as their guide. They are pumped up by unalloyed libido. "I want what I want and I want it now. If you should be in my way, so much the worse for you." This is the credo of the streets and the jungle. Those who ignore it will assuredly be victimized.

In a way we are all victimized. The eyes that avert so that the scene of harassment cannot be viewed, the good Samaritan who has the courage (or is it naïveté?) to get involved and then is stigmatized, the youth who was killed devoid of even the most rudimentary moral standards—all are symbols of a justice system that can't or won't create justice.

For the poor worker—black and white—who is obliged to ride the subway, violence lives a breath away. People stare at their feet, not at the person across the aisle. One learns from years of conditioning. Andy Frederick was like everyone else for most of his life. He got on the subway only because it is the cheapest way to get to work. One day the price was very high.

He maintains that he is no hero. "I'm just an ordinary young man." Certainly, there was nothing ordinary about his behavior. Most New Yorkers ride the subways with blinders on. If you don't, the invasion of graffiti, the jostling and the arrogance of thugs who believe the trains belong to them would be overwhelming.

"Mind your own business," we tell our wives, children, and friends. That's because we care about them. If we weren't so afraid, if there were moral constraints that kept barbarism intact, if the courts recognized a crime is a crime whether committed by a black or a white, we might say, "Mind other people's business."

One day a black worker did just that; he tried to help someone in trouble. I haven't read of William Kunstler's response to Frederick's deeds. I don't have to. In the minds of those trapped by the hobgoblins of race, some explanation will be forthcoming to show that Frederick is not a "true black." In fact, if what the evidence suggests is what actually occurred that fateful day in February, Frederick is a man who brings honor to his race and his community.

Let every subway rider remember that as they stare at the floor of the train.

March 14, 1985

75

What is Behind the Closing
of New York Beaches?

For weeks the red off-limits flags have fluttered along New York and Long Island beaches and the fear of sharks had nothing to do with it. Beach habitués seeking a breath of cool ocean air and a dip in salt water have been driven away by hospital waste that includes syringes and vials of AIDS-tainted blood, washing up on beaches from Fire Island to Sandy Hook. For New Yorkers medical waste on the beach is the theme of the 1988 summer.

In the era of hyperbole, apocalyptic claims are rife. Dr. Stephen C. Joseph, New York City health commissioner, argued that "this period of the 1980s will be remembered as the time the planet struck back. The planet is telling us we can't treat it this way anymore." Virginia Tipple, federal estuaries programs chief, contends, "When the right conditions occur, our garbage comes home to haunt us." Ocean explorers like Jacques Cousteau and Thor Heyerdahl have warned of dead seas due to the dumping of garbage. There is certainly no shortage of claims about the ecological damage that can result from the disposal of waste.

Yet it is interesting that with all the grand claims and supposed investigations, no one has identified the culprit of medical waste on New York's beaches. Is the issue of dumping out of control, beyond government regulation? According to Christopher Daggett, the federal Environmental Protection Agency's regional administrator, the water quality offshore is "generally pretty good." But environmentalists and fishermen dispute this claim. New York, because of the volume of garbage it is forced to dispose of, lack of landfill space, the costs involved, and inertia, does not seem to have an alternative to present practices.

The last few years the primary dumping ground for New York's waste is an area 106 miles out to sea. Despite technical and legal problems associated with this dumping, New York's disposal in this ocean dumping ground has not resulted in any significant environmental or beach-related problems in the past. The question that remains is why should this summer be different from the others.

In an effort to discover who is culpable for the medical-waste products found on New York's beaches, I discussed the issue with ship captains who have worked in New York harbor for years and others working in the field of waste disposal. Their response to the present problem is uniformly the same: it could have been avoided. How it could have been avoided is a matter that relates to present waste-disposal practices in New York and intended or unintended malfeasance.

The blood vials and syringes discovered on local beaches have been traced to New York area hospitals. According to present practice and legal adherence, the medical waste is supposed to be separated from other garbage at a Brooklyn dumpsite and incinerated in a Coney Island or Manhattan incinerator. For some reason that hasn't been happening. While that condition has contributed to the problem, it is still not as significant as the fact that a major company with contractual responsibility for disposing of waste does not have an ocean-going tug capable of reaching the designated ocean dumping site 106 miles into the Atlantic. As a consequence, dumping has been going on thirty to forty miles from our shoreline. It is not coincidental that most of the discovered medical-waste products are two to three months old, since it would take that long for waste dumped at thirty miles out to wash up on our shores.

This isn't the first time illegal dumping practices have occurred, nor is it likely to be the last such episode. The profits to be derived from waste-disposal contracts with the city government are enormous and there is no one available, including the Coast Guard, to monitor the dumping practices of each and every garbage-laden barge. While it may make public officials feel better to attribute generalized blame for the garbage washing up on our beaches, there is blame, and rather specific blame at that, which can be attributed. The dumping of contaminated medical waste is a problem in this city, but it is certainly not an insuperable problem. Dumping in the summer of 1988, which has forced bathers to the shore, can be attributed to disposal of waste at undesignated sites near our beaches and the comingling of medical waste with other garbage products, clear violations of the law.

New York's beaches and swimming areas might well have remained usable this summer if the city administration hadn't converted waste-disposal contracts into a license for polluting our waterways. There is scarcely a person in the waste-disposal business or a city commissioner in this area who doesn't know what practices must be pursued in order to assure relatively clean waterways and clean beaches. That this hasn't occurred indicates contracts haven't been adhered to and officials haven't been vigilant about enforcement of legal dumping practices.

The fear of hepatitis and AIDS has understandably contributed to the general fear of contaminated swimming areas. Yet there is no question that New York's beaches—one of the city's great natural resources—have been made into dumping sites by commercial interests unconcerned about their actions. Even if the beaches are finally cleaned up for the rest of this summer, what remains are city-licensed water fiefdoms that keep every New Yorker hostage to illegal acts and the prospect of future summers with our beaches closed to bathers.

August 3, 1988

Part VI

Education

76

Improving the City's Five Worst
High Schools

Dr. Frank Smith, Jr., the new director of the New York City High Schools, has stated publicly amid great fanfare that he is determined to improve conditions in the city's five worst high schools: Thomas Jefferson, Julia Richman, Eli Whitney, Prospect Heights, and Andrew Jackson. He noted, "We've got to have lessons that make it more worthwhile to be in school than on the streets." One must admire his spirit, but after observing literally dozens of such improvement programs in the city, I am a skeptic about innovation.

To achieve his goals Dr. Smith intends to combine work and study. He refers to planning procedures "with the logic of Rickover's." He waxes eloquent about mini-schools within the ninth grade so that students can spend the school day with the same teachers and students. He refers to a sense of student participation in the affairs of the school. He seems dedicated to a concentration on basic skills, particularly writing. Each of these reforms— notwithstanding some ambiguity about how to introduce them—is unobjectionable. One hopes that the schools will alter the cynical student belief that the classroom is a place to bide one's time.

However, the real key to success in the schools is conspicuously omitted from Dr. Smith's checklist. It is the obvious requisite for every item he considers important and it is the most politically sensitive issue. No matter what reform is introduced it is bound to fail unless there is discipline in the school. That is the sine qua non of education. Without it everything else is window dressing.

But how does one obtain decorous behavior? There must be penalties associated with misbehavior including expulsion. However, the city high schools already have a 35.6 percent dropout rate. Were a behavior code strictly enforced, there is little doubt the drop out rate would reach politically intolerable proportions. Clearly Dr. Smith might be able to refer to improved conditions in the five worst city schools when half the pupils are in attendance and half are on the street.

As long as many teachers, parents, and politicians continue to argue "there is no such thing as a bad kid, there is only a bad school," some schools will remain marginal. Stuyvesant High School isn't an excellent school because of academic innovations; it is a fine school because kids are there to learn. Generally speaking, the teachers don't have to be surrogate guardians, disciplinarians, and baby sitters.

The worst schools in New York are coincidentally the most disruptive. They invariably have the highest truancy rates, the most drug problems, the most damage to school property, and the highest incidence of teacher abuse. Unless and until these matters are addressed, education—even some education—is not likely to occur. It is a charade to argue that student participation, mini-schools, writing skills are the answer to what plagues our schools. The problem is very simply an unwillingness, in some instances an inability, to kick the bums out.

Grand pronouncements about New York public schools won't wash. Most New Yorkers have heard these statements before. It is the will to challenge the prevailing child psychology that is the way to educational improvement. Educational leaders must say we can't teach without order, and order can't be achieved unless you rid us of the "bad apples." That simple nostrum was once axiomatic.

I am a product of New York's public schools. I can vividly recall being alarmed should I get a "pink slip" that would force me to serve a detention after school. I can recall with horror a call to my Mom from my geometry teacher in which I was roundly upbraided for poor grades. These were examples of social controls fostered by the belief that if I did not act properly I could be expelled from school. Despite feeling my adolescent oats, these threats kept my behavior in reasonably well-defined bounds.

At the moment there are virtually no penalties that work. Many teachers are afraid of their students. Many school administrators won't expel disruptive students. And many politicians refer to the dropout rate instead of order in the schools. At the risk of immodest prediction, I'll tell you what will happen to Dr. Smith's reforms. They will receive high grades at first. Students will love the mini-school concept. But when the behavior problems aren't remedied, an educator will suggest the transfer of disruptive students out of the targeted schools. If that happens the project will be deemed a success; if not, conditions will return to normal, the pronouncements will have been forgotten, Dr. Smith will have moved on to a new job, and the five worst schools will still be the five worst schools.

September 13, 1986

77

A Proposal for the New Chancellor

Here is some advice for the new chancellor of the New York City schools that would unquestionably assist in his quest for educational improvement: eliminate all special programs from the regular school day. If such a recommendation were accepted, there would be additional resources to pursue the primary goals of the schools, namely, the basics to which educators of all political persuasions now give lip service.

While such a proposal will have detractors, particularly those with a stake in the retention of these programs, the effect on the schools' curriculum can only be salutary. Consider the real meaning of this retrenchment. Alcohol and drug-abuse programs, environmental studies, sex education, racial-awareness programs, peace or nuclear education, driver education, AIDS programs, which presently encroach on the valuable time needed to teach reading comprehension, math skills, writing competence, science, history, would be eliminated as an intrusion on basic skills and knowledge.

By eliminating these special programs the chancellor would also be eliminating the source of much political disagreement in the schools. There is, for example, the unresolved issue of sex education in classrooms and the nature of that instruction. Without such subjects, moral instruction would return to home or religious institutions where many believe it belongs.

It is also the case that these subjects are the target of special interests and as a consequence the source of misrepresentation. AIDS-program instructors, to cite one case, continue to assert that heterosexuals are as likely to contract the disease as homosexuals, a claim that defies the evidence. Of course, when schools are used to promote special interests, misrepresentation is to be expected.

Lest it be argued that the elimination of these courses and programs deprive students in some incalculable way, I would urge the extension of after-school activities to encompass these activities. That way special programs can be retained and the basics can still be restored to the primary position in the curriculum that they deserve. Moreover, it would be interesting to see how many parents would take advantage of these programs if they were deemed voluntary.

The key to this proposal is the restoration of basic skills and subjects to the core of the educational mission. In so doing, student performance on basic-skills tests is bound to improve. It is axiomatic that students tend to test well on subjects they have studied. That American students do not score as well on math tests as their Japanese and European counterparts can be attributed in large measure to the fact that most Americans as a rule can graduate from high school with fewer than two courses in mathematics, while Japanese and Europeans must take four courses in math to satisfy graduation requirements.

For more than two decades the approach to education in our schools resembles a supermarket where the item purchased is based on preference, with each commodity perceived as having equal value. Under this condition it is hardly surprising that students gravitate to the subjects of least difficulty. It explains why science and math literacy is in an abysmal state. It further explains why the United States may be less competitive than some of our trade associates.

Yet the timing for change is propitious. Educators of all persuasions contend something is wrong with our schools, with evidence for this claim found in the woeful performance of students on tests of basic skills. By giving students a chance to learn what is necessary to cope in the modern age, the chancellor will be heralded as the St. George of education slaying the dragon of philistinism. Surely there will be those arrayed against him who will raise the banner of relevance, but he must stay the course if he wants to do the best by our youngsters and the most for our schools.

March 8, 1988

78

McGuffey's Readers and Moral Education

It now appears as if everyone is talking about values in our schools. Let me set the record straight and talk about moral principles. What is generally proposed by new-age prophets like Governor Mario Cuomo is yet another rehearsal of moral relativism, exercises in situational morality. However, it is clear that the moral confusion in our schools is due to the fact that few concrete proposals have emerged on what to do. At the moment Professor Louis Kohlberg and his taxonomy of values clarification rules the cultural roost. A substitute is certainly needed if a modicum of sound thinking is to be introduced into the curriculum.

My proposal to address this issue is the reintroduction of *McGuffey's Eclectic Readers* into New York's schools. For approximately one hundred years starting in 1836 these books were used as basal readers training more than a billion Americans in character development. William Holmes McGuffey, originator of the series, did not expect young students to ponder hypothetical situations and decide what is good and bad. His text made crystal clear what virtues must be encouraged and the vices that should be spurned. In fact, the moral content in these texts was viewed as a necessary requisite to assimilate newcomers into the rapidly expanding democracy of the nineteenth and early twentieth centuries.

The message was bold and direct. One *Reader* suggests to students:

> Your parents are kind to send you to school. If you are good, and if you try to learn, your teacher will love you, and you will please your parents. Be kind to all, and do not waste your time in school. When you go home, you may ask your parents to get you a Second Reader.

In one primer, Mary—the central actor—demonstrates many noble traits. She is kind to her friends; she helps a blind man cross the road; she often sacrifices her own pleasures for the benefit of others. Her companion Tom "will not rob a bird's nest. He is too kind to do so." For the characters in *McGuffey's Readers* good deeds have notable rewards. When a young boy uses his savings to pay for the windowpane shattered by his snowball, he is rewarded with a job and, eventually a partnership in the store. When another youngster gives his money to the needy instead of buying books he covets, the boy ends up with the poor family's gratitude and the books, purchased by his proud father, who notes, "Be thus ever ready to help the poor, and the wretched, and distressed; and every year of your life will be a happy New Year!"

As virtue is rewarded, misdeeds are punished. When an insolent youngster pelts a stranger with stones, the unfamiliar visitor turns out to be a relative whose presents go to only his well-behaved relations. Ill-mannered kids are always punished whether by the force of circumstances or God's will. Only after punishment and repentance do ill-mannered children know happiness. The virtue of hard work and learning are also emphasized as rewards in themselves. In one story a girl tells her mother and father that she is happier when she spends the evening sewing than in recreational activity. The child says, "It is because we have all been doing something useful tonight."

Some school systems have decided to use these textbooks in the classroom once again. My guess is that in these schools the value of honesty, courage, and industry is emphasized when it had been ignored heretofore. These simple *Readers* provide perspective on the cultural tradition that gave past generations moral guidance. They are unambiguous about right and wrong, good and bad. They are basal texts for those learning to read and they are catalysts for the character development of all children.

Admittedly there will be naysayers who argue these books are hopelessly out of date. There are other critics who contend that our world is more complex than the past, making nineteenth-century moral messages inappropriate. But wherever there are serious educators concerned about the inculcation of moral principles, it is worth recounting a sermon from one *McGuffey's Reader*:

> Beautiful faces are they that wear
> The light of pleasant spirit there;
> Beautiful hands are they that do
> Deeds that are noble, good and true;
> Beautiful feet are they that go
> Swiftly to lighten another's woe.

November 6, 1986

79

Barbarism in a New York High School

There are times when a story appears in a newspaper that is so astonishing one doesn't know whether to laugh or cry. It has been reported that Park West High School in the heart of New York City is a place where students routinely carry guns and knives in their bookbags. "Violence erupts over even such trifling items as train passings." Last week a seventeen-year-old student slashed another student with a machete.

In response to these brutal conditions, the director of the Board of Education's office of school safety, Bruce Irushalmi, said that the violence at Park West was "very disturbing" and the number of weapons "used inside and outside the school is excessive." Excessive? That word jumped off the page when I read the article about Park West High School. Is there a number of weapons that would be acceptable?

The principal of the high school made even more fatuous remarks, if that is possible. Despite the reports of violence, he said the school is "safe." In virtually the same breath he claimed "the level of violence is nothing new." According to Edward Morris, the principal, "We're dealing with all the malaise of society and 3000 individuals. The school is a microcosm of society." Well, if this is a microcosm of society, I wonder why everyone doesn't carry a machete and a .22 caliber revolver in his briefcase.

Morris's comments get better or worse depending on your perspective. "Kids," he notes, "have been bringing weapons to school for years. It's almost a habit to carry weapons. This is not unique to Park West. Because Morris has been the principal since the school opened in 1978, one must ask why he has tolerated these conditions. Is he trying to argue you can't break students of their "habit" of carrying weapons?

What brought this issue to the attention of the press was an all-day sit-in at the school by several hundred recently arrived students from the Dominican Republic. They said they would not attend classes until the school's security was assured. This seems like a reasonable request even for a school that has an "excessive number" of weapons. However, what must be understood is that the school resembles an armed camp more than a learning environment. On a recent search of students deemed suspicious, knives of all descriptions, a loaded revolver, a meat cleaver, brass knuckles were found. Some teachers claim the majority of students carry weapons of some kind.

It is interesting, of course, that students from the Dominican Republic should find their homeland less barbaric than conditions in New York. For youngsters in this Hell's Kitchen neighborhood, violence is a way of life. Miguel Cruz, a student who transferred from the school, said, "I was going to school with a knife because the others always went to school with a knife."

It is simply mind-boggling that some people have been reduced to accepting violence as a condition in the schools with knives as accoutrements like blackboards, chalk, and textbooks. Even more remarkable is a principal who denies the problem and then contradicts himself. What kind of educator can accept these conditions? Then there is the equally remarkable person in charge of school safety who claims the number of weapons is "excessive." Perhaps someone dealing with the problem of school safety everyday is numbed by the experience. Or perhaps someone selected for this job has to be numb before being appointed to the job.

Park West High School puts on center stage everything that is wrong with the city's schools. There is no accountability among administrators, teachers, or students. There is the acceptance of barbarism as a way of life. There is no attempt to search every student every day—for fear, I suspect, that such a practice will arouse civil libertarians. There appears to be no understanding at the Board of Education of the severity of the problem or what school safety entails.

In the last analysis the group I feel most sorry for are those Dominicans who came to this country seeking a better life for their children. What they find instead is assault, robbery, slashing, even murder in our schools. "The rockets' red glare" in our National Anthem depicted a scene from the war of 1812 when courage and patriotism were on display. In some of New York's schools this expression is a literal view of daily violence. The rockets are guns held by adolescents and the red is blood spilled on the floor of our school buildings.

December 31, 1987

80

The Study of Learning Styles

The educational establishment never ceases to challenge my credulity. Recently the New York State Board of Regents appointed a special panel to explore the proposition that blacks and other minority students have "learning styles" that are different from whites. Presumably if this determination is made, teaching techniques will be introduced to accommodate the unique learning styles.

Creation of this panel came in response to a state-sponsored booklet on "learning styles" that some educators have described as racist and others have defended as a valuable insight. State Education Commissioner Dr. Thomas Sobel, caught in a political vise, organized the panel to advise the regents on the ways in which biological, social, and cultural differences affect learning.

However, whatever the determination, a storm is brewing. Louis Grumet, executive director of the State School Boards Association, said, "A study that conclusively proved that there was a connection between ethnicity and education would cause you to separate those kids for their own enrichment into separate ethnic groups—and that is opposed to everything this country stands for." Assemblywoman Cynthia Jenkins of Queens contends that "God didn't give out brains on the basis of color. What are you going to tell teachers that have Asian, Black, White and Hispanic kids—that they're going to have four different lesson plans?"

Passages in the booklet, written by Education Department staff members, asserted that "children's racial, ethnic and emotional backgrounds and cultures influence the manner in which they learn concepts and process information." The distinction drawn was between inferential reasoning and deductive or inductive reasoning and, get this, a tendency on the part of blacks "to approximate space, number and time instead of aiming for complete accuracy." In order to mollify both sides in this controversy, Dr. Sobel organized a review of the matter by experts in "biophysical functions which affect

183

learning, as well as experts in cultural, historical and psychological traits, which are also important to learning and success.'' But once the experts appeared on the scene, Dr. Sobel came to the conclusion it would be be best to drop the review completely.

What remains is a panel to examine teaching techniques for what is presumed to be distinct learning styles. Yet no matter how you slice it, this examination cannot have a salubrious effect on education. Recognition of unique learning styles based on race and ethnicity invites bigotry. Moreover, how can any educator legitimate a ''learning style'' that approximates space, numbers, and time? Is it appropriate to say to a black youngster who uses ''inferential reasoning'' that two plus two is almost equal to five? The easiest way to ensure the backwardness of any group is to dignify this so-called learning style.

On the face of it, learning styles are analogous to lifestyles. One lives a life, not a lifestyle, and one learns or doesn't learn. Surely some people are smarter than others and some learn more than others. Some students work hard to learn and some don't care to learn. If the Board of Regents wants to spend the taxpayers' money on a project that is worthwhile, it ought to find out which schools and teachers get the most out of their students regardless of race, class, or family background. Instead of postulating different learning styles for blacks, it would be useful to determine why school achievement is often stigmatized in black communities. It might be equally useful to determine why many Asian students facing racial difference and language barriers do manage to succeed in disproportionate numbers in American schools.

There are a growing number of so-called experts in the field of learning methods. However, no one has yet improved on the need for discipline—an inner desire to succeed—which manifests itself in the seat of one's pants meeting the seat of a chair consistently. That sense of discipline must be reinforced with teachers who assign and grade homework, with parents and guardians who insist on study, and with a national culture that puts a premium on learning. All the panels in the world studying every dimension of biophysical functions cannot possibly come up with a more commonsensical approach to achievement than study habits that are cultivated early and reinforced throughout one's school years.

January 21, 1988

81

How to Find More Good Teachers

It is hard to believe that seven years ago, after the demographic trends militated against the need for teachers, there is now a teacher shortage. In New York City alone, the Board of Education is scrambling to fill 600 vacancies. Most of them have been filled temporarily waiving some hiring requirements. But it is obvious that these short-term measures will be inadequate if demand for teachers continues to exceed supply, and if the pressure on demand is exacerbated by a call for small class size, special education programs, and rigorous employment requirements.

Although the shortage represents an immediate problem that must be addressed, it also is an opportunity to refashion the teaching job and appeal to people who would not, under ordinary circumstances, consider teaching as a career.

If one were to believe everything that is said about college graduates today, you would assume that each and every graduate wants to be in business and that pursuit of wealth is the only goal in life. That view is neither flattering nor accurate, albeit there must be financial rewards in teaching commensurate with the responsibility and the new pressures on demand.

It seems to me that a seven-part recruitment program must be considered to attract talented people. The first and perhaps the most important condition is an assurance to future teachers, particularly those slated for urban schools, that their safety will be assured. Invariably, candidates for positions ask about their safety in "tough schools."

It seems to me that it should be sufficient for a teacher to know his discipline; the teacher shouldn't have to be trained in Kung Fu. If what is required for teaching is combat experience, then a Marine battalion should be hired to teach in our schools. That, by the way, is not such a bad idea.

A second reform is that the graduate students with a 3.5 grade average or better should be actively recruited. One way to do that is to waive "education-course" requirements that often discourage the serious student from pursuing a career in teaching. With bright students, there must also be a willingness to consider approaches to education that do not square with the prevailing teaching methodology.

According to present guidelines for teaching, Socrates would violate every regulation in the books. We've simply got to make it easy for Socrates to teach in our schools. A third idea is to have part-time instructors who are homemakers or involved in military service considered. It is far better to have a talented person for part of the school day than a deadhead for a full day.

Fourth, on the other side of the ledger is a person who ordinarily teaches nine months a year, for what is generally considered an inadequate salary. One way to improve teacher salaries significantly is to offer teachers a "full-year salary"—representing an immediate 25 percent increase in income—for a full year's work.

Fifth, as a lure to undergraduates who consider future career options on the basis of first-year salaries, it is desirable to increase the salary in entry-level teaching positions from an average of $15,000 to $20,000. The $5,000 differential may not be a strong magnet for new teachers, but at the margin it could have some bearing on recruitment efforts.

Sixth, it is imperative that the authorities in education begin to think of their jobs as a genuine profession. Teaching has been so culturally downgraded that it is often equated with babysitting. I would recommend an award for teachers comparable to the Nobel Prize, with a similar monetary benefit. The prize could be given each year when a blue-ribbon panel is convinced the recipients have engaged in those activities that extend educational opportunities to students or expand the horizons of knowledge.

Last, I would recommend the establishment of a merit pay system. Despite all the arguments I've heard to the contrary, it seems to me that fair-minded and sensible people can establish a system for rewarding those members of the profession whose work goes beyond the call of duty, whose students perform at a level beyond expectations, and whose dedication to the job is unquestionable.

Although I'm confident these reforms could make a difference in dealing with the teacher-supply issue, they may not be sufficient to attract some of the most talented students into the teaching profession.

That can be done only when there is the widely held belief that teachers are important for our nation's competitive advantage, that they shape the future course of our history and mold the minds that will lead us. At the moment, these are empty clichés. The real challenge for educators is to give these arguments meaning again.

September 11, 1985

82

Call a Lawyer: The Obvious Thing to Do

An irate parent writing in the *New York Times* says that his fourteen-year-old, who happens to be dyslexic, can receive proper attention only if she is classified as "emotionally disturbed" by the Board of Education. If parental consent is given to this newfound malady she will be placed in a mini-school when there is a favorable teacher-student ratio. I don't blame this parent for being angry. The Byzantine decisions at the board often defy logic.

However, acting in his daughter's behalf, this parent says, "I have done the obvious things—engaged a lawyer, laid on outside experts." What I find particularly revealing about this comment is the equation between "obvious things" and engaging the services of a lawyer. Think about it. In a way remarkably more true now than, say, thirty years ago, any real or perceived grievance necessitates legal intervention. But why should that be the case or the obvious thing to do?

In this instance the obvious thing to do is to assist one's daughter in the painstaking chore of reading at home. Instead of spending one's resources on legal counsel in an effort to redress absurd Board of Education policies, it seems to me that the issue can be dealt with directly by doing whatever is possible to provide educational service at home. That is certainly going to assist the young lady in question more than legal briefs and court action.

So litigious have we become as a society that seeking legal assistance for a problem is a reflexive response. Rather than consider what we can do to remedy the issue, the lawyer has become the social salve of the first resort. What this means, of course, is that many people have adopted a process for the adjudication of knotty problems that takes the grievants themselves out of the solution. Lawyers are presumably there to solve our problems or to give us satisfaction. Here is yet another reason why so many people describe their condition as one of powerlessness, yet in invoking legal minds they are contributing to their very complaint.

Let me state the obvious by noting that life is imperfect. There will always be unfairness; there can never be genuine equality. In fact the closer one comes to a fair social order, the more marginal differences are exaggerated. In legal disputes one is dealing not only with objective conditions but with perceptions. Believing you are aggrieved is as exasperating as actually being aggrieved. These concerns haven't changed over time. There are and probably always will be people who are legitimately angry or who justify their anger by using the social system as a scapegoat.

What is different now, however, is the army of lawyers ready to pounce on these concerns for financial gain, a gain I should add that is usually not paid by the litigants but by the rest of us in the form of higher insurance rates, higher taxes, and higher prices for products and services. It is now so customary to call on a lawyer to remedy a grievance that it is the obvious thing to do. Yet the price we pay in losing control over events and in raising the ante on other expenses is usually ignored.

Problem-solving skills are like muscles that will atrophy unless they are used. By asking lawyers to flex their mental muscles for us, we lose sight of our ability to intervene in our own behalf. We assume that along with health problems that require a physician for a cure, social problems require "experts" for their solution. Yet in most instances one doesn't have to be an expert to solve a personal problem.

I am distressed that a young girl who is dyslexic must agree to an emotional problem in order to get the kind of attention in our schools she deserves. Clearly Mom and Dad should be getting more for their tax dollars than has heretofore been the case. But it is still not obvious to me that a lawyer will solve this problem. A lawyer can't teach the girl how to read and probably can't effect changes in an ossified educational bureaucracy. All a lawyer can do is charge for services and give the girl's parents some psychic satisfaction they are not getting at the moment. Should this litigation be successful, we will all pay for the lawyer's fee and the results of the court action.

October 30, 1986

83

Fixing New York Schools

New York City's schools are not an unmitigated disaster. After all, New York students still win a disproportionate number of Westinghouse science awards, "the best and brightest" still go to Stuyvesant and Bronx Science high schools, and dedicated teachers can still be found in the system. None of these assets, however, can offset the egregious characteristics in the schools.

The relatively low scores on standardized tests, the disciplinary problems, the inability of most high school graduates from five designated schools to pass an eighth-grade math exam that would have guaranteed their employment in a New York bank—all speak directly to the issue of school quality.

Yet while everyone has an opinion about our schools, very little in the way of discernible improvement has occurred. It seems to me the reason for this is obvious: almost all educators ignore the conditions that are universally known to foster sound schools. Whether one refers to the articles of a liberal such as Ronald Edmonds or a conservative such as William Bennett, secretary of education, the advice is the same.

Good schools depend on parental involvement. Parents must have a role in the establishment of the curriculum, in disciplinary procedures, and in the selection of a principal. I've met parents who were complacent about the schools, but I've never met parents who didn't want the best possible education for their child.

Good schools require a consistent pattern of expectations. Students should know that if you don't score at the twelfth-grade level on a normed reading test, you can't graduate from high school. In example after example, educational literature shows that learning across racial and economic lines occurs most effectively when schools have a high level of expectation. There is no reason to believe American students can't perform as well as Japanese students on standardized tests if we expect as much from our youngsters as Japanese authorities do from theirs.

Good schools need strong leaders, principals with the courage of their convictions. While it is often difficult to find such people, they do exist. If most New York principals were unshackled from political concerns so that they could focus on educational matters, one might be surprised at how much talent is already available.

Good schools require an emphasis on basic skills over all other school activities. With the schools as social cures of the last resort, an enormous block of time is spent on drug education, driver education, sex education, and now AIDS education. Whenever the society has an issue it doesn't know how to address, it is dumped into the school system. Is it any wonder most students can't do a long-division problem or locate Brazil on a map?

Good schools must have an orderly climate without being oppressive. You can't learn if everyone shouts at once. You can't run a school when thugs parade up and down the corridors intimidating serious students. And a school cannot possibly function well when intelligent discourse is degraded by ignorant criticism. The number-one math student in the school should be accorded the same respect as the high scorer on the basketball team.

Good schools monitor their students' progress frequently. The only way to measure achievement is through testing. A grade on a test is admittedly inexact, but it is the only way to determine what students know. In the age where educators consider themselves Anna Freud, the psychological well-being of children is accorded more importance than their skills and knowledge. Of course, what these post-Freudians don't understand is that the deepest scars are left with those students who graduate from our schools despite an inability to read, write, and compute.

If what I've suggested is known to be true, educational authorities in this city have a responsibility to create these conditions in schools deemed failures. Instead of turning all the schools topsy-turvy—something my emotional side would be inclined to do—it makes sense to select the "three worst high schools" and use them as a laboratory for improvement.

Give the parents an expansive role in the school program, establish a high level of achievement for graduation, hire a strong principal and give him the latitude to do the job, place an emphasis on basic skills to the virtual exclusion of other subjects, make sure the environment is orderly, and test often. My guess is some New York schools could be excellent schools in a short time. I may be wrong, but is there anything to lose in trying?

November 7, 1987

Part VII

Several Proposals to Aid New York

84

Reclaiming New York from the Barbarians

Mario Merola, the Bronx district attorney, stood on the steps of the Bronx County Courthouse, making a speech as the television cameras were rolling. I don't know what he was saying because my attention focused on the columns and walls behind Merola. They were covered with graffiti.

The edifice that stands as the symbol and repository of law in this borough has been blemished by an act of indiscriminate violence against one of its cherished institutions. So accustomed are we to seeing graffiti that it is hardly noticed; it is certainly not noticed as an act of violence.

Then it struck me. How can we let a courthouse be overrun by the barbarians? If it means repainting the façade of that building every day or having a twenty-four-hour guard detail, that courthouse must be reclaimed from the clutches of barbarians who do not respect the law or public property.

In fact, if I let my thoughts wander, it would be enormously beneficial if the city could reclaim a number of public institutions from the control of barbarism. Why is it that a law-abiding, tax-paying member of this community cannot safely use a public restroom in this entire city? Public restrooms are controlled by vagrants, hoods, and drug dealers. A normal person wouldn't use a public facility even if his bladder were about to burst.

It seems to me that as a symbolic act of reclaiming this city from those engaged in despoiling it, one men's and one women's facility should be secured. They should be cleaned, fumigated, and patrolled.

I would also contend that one park should be selected as a site reclaimed by decent people. Drug dealers would be banned. Even if it means arresting every dealer three times a day or having a regular canine patrol, one park should be secured.

One public waiting room in a train station should be freed of vagrants and converted into a place where the stench of urine and sleeping forms on the benches aren't present.

Keep in mind that I am referring to one park, one courthouse, one urinal, one waiting room. As much as I might like to see it, the idea of reclaiming all the city's institutions from the assault of barbarism is beyond our capacity or perhaps beyond our will.

Nonetheless, the reclamation projects I've suggested serve an important symbolic purpose. They would demonstrate that this city administration recognizes the need to protect the rights of decent people. Moreover, reclaiming these institutions would indicate that public facilities are not only for vagrants and the criminal element. As hard as it may be to believe, those restrooms in our subways belong to every New Yorker.

Yet we have allowed our sensibilities to slide down the slippery slope of least resistance. We have not challenged the barbarians. Instead, we look the other way or walk around the perimeter of a park or try to find a men's room in a midtown hotel or wait for a train in Grand Central Station at Zaro's.

A victory for barbarism isn't complete, but who can deny the victory. Decent people have been defeated as one public institution after another falls under the sway of undesirables. From a strategic point of view the average person must do more than contain the losses; the person should engage in "rollback."

New York needs a citizens campaign to reacquire control over one institution a month for one year. This should be done with fanfare. The mayor might even derive political capital from the gesture. There have been days when I'd vote for anyone who could provide a clean, secure restroom in midtown.

The most important dimension of this reclamation program is the announcement that this city doesn't belong to those who deface, despoil, or destroy. New York was built by poor, hardworking people who asked for little more than a chance to get ahead and returned the opportunity to live and work here with gratitude. We can't let that convenant with the city be rescinded by a barbarity that has come to dominate public places.

February 10, 1987

85

The Grass Is Not Greener in the Suburbs

Fifty miles from the epicenter of New York, highway traffic crawls at a glacial pace. The country road that was once a haven for disenchanted city drivers has been converted into a traffic bottleneck. Businesses that moved out of New York to escape the traffic find that it has followed them to the outer suburbs. The result of these conditions is that the metropolitan region's roads have been overwhelmed.

From 1980 to the present, the suburbs have gained 763,000 jobs compared with New York City's gain of 306,000. Jobs in the 'burbs involve new commuting patterns with every member of the family reliant on the automobile. The number of cars in suburbia far outstrips population growth.

In the New York region traffic is a reflection of economic development in the suburbs. Nearly 80 percent of Long Islanders work in Nassau or Suffolk counties. More residents of Rockland County work in New Jersey or Westchester County than in Manhattan. In fact Manhattan is not the magnet for economic activity it once was. The Long Island Expressway is as much a highway for intra-Long Island traffic as for commutation from Long Island to New York.

According to planners this trend will ultimately strangulate the near suburbs forcing people to move into rural areas. Yet there is an alternative—one might even describe it as an opportunity. City officials should encourage suburbanites to move to New York. After all, New York does have a mass transit system that could be effective. New Yorkers are not dependent on the automobile, even though that is hard to believe on Friday afternoon at the entrance to the Holland Tunnel.

The key to this campaign is the effort to control crime. Despite the lack of amenities and the traffic crawl, suburbia does offer streets relatively free of violent crime. Most suburban residents are willing to tolerate a great deal in order to avoid the city's violence. That is the nub of the issue and the matter on which city officials seem to be inert in addressing.

The problems in the suburbs are not presented to suggest that suburbia is less desirable than urban areas or that the lower rate of crime indicates that suburbs are preferable to the city. New York's metropolitan area has a range of living environments. However, it is fair to claim that many people in the suburbs can afford and would prefer to live in the city—even in the outer boroughs—if crime could be brought under control. The key to broadening the tax base is encouraging suburbanites to relocate to New York.

There is no major elixir for bringing about this result. However, congestion in the suburbs could be a catalyst for reexamination of suburban living. One expects traffic on Fifth Avenue; it is somewhat unnerving to discover bumper-to-bumper traffic on the Cross Westchester Expressway. While there has been some "in-migration" to New York from the suburbs in the last two decades, it is relatively minor compared to what might have occurred if the city were a desirable living alternative.

The rejuvenation of marginal areas from Washington Heights to the Grand Concourse could be activated with the surge of suburbanite relocation. That challenge should be embraced by the city administration. It is one thing to talk about New York's virtues; it is quite another to recognize what is needed so that decent, tax-paying people will live here.

Traffic and high housing costs were the factors that led many of New York's businesses to relocate to the suburbs. Now some of those suburban business officials have learned that the grass isn't always greener outside New York City. A portion of these businesses will move farther away; others could conceivably move to New York. The lines are drawn; the environment for new business and new residents is competitive. It is incumbent on New York's municipal officials to begin a long, undeviating, relentless war against crime so the city can once again be the place where most people in this region want to live.

August 10, 1988

86

Banning the Bike

The bicycle has led a charmed life. Almost everyone gets one; it doesn't rely on imported oil; one doesn't need a license to drive it. On the other hand, the bicycle has become a pedestrian and traffic menace in New York. This point was finally recognized by Mayor Koch when he announced a three-month experimental ban on bicycles in midtown Manhattan.

The history of this decision is worth examining. In the mayoralty campaign of 1965 William Buckley suggested that the way to alleviate Manhattan traffic was to rely on city-owned bicycles that could be picked up and deposited at designated locations. At the time it was difficult to know whether or not Buckley's tongue was in his cheek.

There are New Yorkers who believe that this city once named New Amsterdam can resemble its European sister city of Amsterdam with bicyclists competing with cars for street space. In fact, in 1980, during Mayor Koch's first term, lanes were installed on midtown avenues in the hope that bicycles would be accorded the same respect as autos. This was Koch's fantasy of turning New York into a cyclist's Beijing.

New York, however, is neither Beijing nor Amsterdam. It is a city that relies on its own idiosyncratic energy. Trying to convert New York into a bicyclist's paradise is like trying to build the Empire State Building on the marshes of Secaucus. To his credit, the mayor has finally come to his senses by scrapping his bicycle lanes on Manhattan's most congested streets and banning bicycles in midtown Manhattan.

The decision is not without its detractors. While it will most certainly result in rider and pedestrian safety, bicycle advocacy groups and messenger services are angry. As one might guess, a spokesman for the New York Cycle Club said, "Instead of initiating efforts to reduce the use of the internal combustion engines and encourage the use of non-polluting self-propelled vehicles, they come up with this hare-brained scheme."

Admittedly, the bicycle is often safer than a subway ride, cheaper than a taxi, and cleaner than a car. Nonetheless, it can imperil pedestrians and be a catalyst for traffic accidents. It is hard to find a New Yorker who looks exclusively to the left to track oncoming traffic; one has been conditioned to look for the speeding cyclist going in the opposite direction. A cabbie is not only cautious of New Jersey drivers, he's learned to be apprehensive of cyclists who aren't always easily visible and don't signal when making a turn.

Since 1980 the number of New Yorkers who commute by bicycle into Manhattan below 60th Street has increased by 42.5 percent, to an estimated 30,000 cyclists. It is also noteworthy that 59 percent of the 19,148 traffic-violation summonses issued in 1986 went to recreational bicyclists and messengers. Bike riders are fond of saying the activity provides better exercise than a health club. That may be true, but those bicycles also cause accidents and jeopardize pedestrian safety.

For the bicycle afficionado I say ride in the park. For the health enthusiasts I say trade in your two-wheeler for a stationary bike. For the commuter I say try the subway; with 30,000 additional riders there may be safety in numbers. For the bike messenger I say get a license and pay a fine if you break the law. Since bike messengers travel at speeds faster than automobiles they should be subject to the same rules of the road as car drivers.

The mayor should do something to curb the inflow of cars, taxis, and trucks that are choking midtown traffic, but it doesn't help matters to have bicycles riding alongside automobiles. Three people died last year because of cyclist collisions with pedestrians; scores of others were injured. Nine people were killed in accidents between bicycles and motor vehicles. This is not a laughing matter.

New York should restrict cars coming into Manhattan. It should also restrict bicycles. I, for one, applaud Mayor Koch's decision. But I still don't understand why this born-and-bred New Yorker ever believed our streets could be converted into those of Beijing.

September 15, 1987

87

Traffic and Crime in New York City

It is seemingly ironic that the incoming chief of the Parking Violations Bureau, Thomas McEnery, was obliged to pay $900 in overdue parking fines and late penalties during the past year. In fact, his latest payment of $135 was made three days after Mayor Koch appointed him the new parking commissioner. Most of the violations were incurred by his three children while they were living at the family home in Jackson Heights.

While these infractions don't really suggest anything about McEnery's qualifications for his new job, they do serve notice about the perverse way law enforcement is conducted in this city. McEnery's children are in their teen years and early twenties. As a responsible parent—which I assume he is—he was probably a bit reluctant to see his children use public transportation on late-night visits to Manhattan. The car became an indispensable means of conveyance.

However, taking a car to Manhattan means that you are asking for trouble. The $900 in traffic violations attest to the fact the McEnery children found it. There are two crimes that New York City policemen are vigilant about: traffic violations and serious felonies, for example, murder and rape. Everything in between is regarded as part of the city ambience. The reaction to a stolen purse or a mugging is instructive. Most cops say, "What can you do? This is New York!"

Yet it may well be the case that a lower level of vigilance over minor traffic violations that has been the case heretofore and a higher level of vigilance over street crime could reduce the incentive for using a car to get to Manhattan. If one didn't have to worry about getting mugged on a subway or robbed on the streets, there might be some willingness to leave that car garaged in Jackson Heights.

I would propose that McEnery and Police Commissioner Benjamin Ward call a moratorium on traffic violations for a one-month period. During that time every effort should be made to encourage people to use public transportation with the supposition that the police department will declare war against subway and street hoods. Instead of the usual "There isn't much we can do about this sort of thing," every cop would be authorized to arrest and prosecute to the full extent of the law the robbers and muggers who prowl the streets and subways.

Although the city administration derives significant revenue from traffic violations, those tickets are a form of harassment against those who are generally law-abiding citizens. It simply makes no sense to harass those who pay their taxes and obey the laws and ignore those parasites who live off other people. At the Traffic Violations Hearing Office at Astor Place, one generally finds middle-class people who are trying to make a living contesting a ticket into which they were euchered.

It is difficult living in this city under the best of circumstances, but when you get a ticket for double parking because your bladder is about to explode and legal spaces are unavailable to park your car, there is a basic injustice. There are few matters that can irritate a New Yorker more than getting a ticket for doing what any sensible person would normally do. It is virtually impossible to be a driver in Manhattan who hasn't had a traffic violation. Those red-faced people on the streets cursing at meter maids and cops are simply part of the city landscape.

My proposal is no panacea. If McEnery is truly lax in prosecuting traffic offenders, gridlock could be the result. On the other hand, using every available law-enforcement officer to clean up the streets could, in time, reduce midtown traffic congestion. It seems to warrant a try. McEnery's personal experience would indicate that even our public officials charged with upholding the law can't avoid traffic violations.

In the last analysis what New York requires is an appreciation of the synergy between traffic and crime. That may not be an easy sell, but for those who are tortured by parking tickets and fearful of using public transportation, it would be best to be lenient about traffic violations and rigid about street and subway crime.

April 19, 1988

88

Union Square Park Should Be Closed

The New York City Parks Department has spent several million dollars renovating Union Square Park. From what I have observed, this department should be commended: the statues have been cleaned; sods of thick grass have been placed on the barren ground. To the outsiders, unfamiliar with this park's history, the renovation must appear a blessing. For the harried New Yorker the quietude in the park is a necessary respite from the city's frantic pace.

However, things are not always as they appear. Union Square Park may have a new face but its soul is encumbered with drugs. For the last ten years, until it was closed for renovation, this park was the drug distribution center in the city. On any given day one could find dozens of pushers plying their narcotics. There was nothing surreptitious about the sales. Everyone in the neighborhood is familiar with what was going on.

The pushers regard apprehension as an overhead expense. A misdemeanor offense for drug possession and sale might lead to a $100 fine. Since most of these pushers earn $1,500 a day on the average, this is a modest fee to pay for the continuation of their trade.

At the moment the pushers stand on the other side of the street away from the surveillance of the police officers now assigned to the park. They still meet addicts to consummate deals. Some have moved downtown to Washington Square Park, encroaching on the ''upscale'' pushers in Greenwich Village. The residents and storekeepers of the Union Square area are convinced it is only a matter of time before the pushers will be back in the park. They are not so much resentful as they are resigned to that eventuality.

There are no simple solutions to the problem. Drugs are a scourge in this city; their use seems beyond the control of the criminal-justice system. Moreover, while politicians give lip service to the menace drugs represent, they have not taken the necessary steps to curb distribution.

I doubt if it will discourage pushers if Union Square Park is closed. After all, the drugs will still be available on the streets; the junkies will still search for a fix. However, the result of keeping the park closed would be a modest tribute to the parks' employees who worked so hard and well to bring natural beauty to this city. The squirrels would benefit and people in nearby high rises and those buildings about to be completed could appreciate the contrast in view that the park would provide.

Admittedly, this is a public facility available to all city residents. But compare Union Square Park before the renovation to Gramercy Square Park that is closed to the public. The former was in ruin; the latter is one of the delightful garden spots in the city. If Gramercy Park were open to the public the pushers would undoubtedly preempt the park for themselves, quickly transforming it into a garbage heap.

The idea of a public facility presuppoes open access. But in this city openness—especially to pushers—means ruin. Decent people can't use the parks; they are the targets of abuse, if not direct violence. Nonetheless, parks do have a role in the city; they stand in stark relief to cement and car exhausts.

It is my contention that this one public park on Union Square should be closed, a testimony to order and civic virtue. Many egalitarians will argue that my position is elitist, that by keeping a public facility closed to the public there is a violation of trust. But isn't it a violation of trust to use tax-levied funds to repair a park only to have it converted into an urban wasteland? Let me assure you that if you want the blossoms to fall, the benches to be destroyed, the grass uprooted, then give Union Square Park back to the pushers.

September 26, 1985

89

A Plan for Late-Night Subway Use

Anyone who uses the New York subway system after 11:00 P.M. is either intrepid, without travel alternatives, looking for trouble, or plain dumb. By any standard, including performance in the past, the transit system is inefficient and dangerous. For years city officials have asked policy experts to recommend solutions. A decade ago a Rand study was completed. While the advice in this report may have had some utility, it is now collecting dust on a municipal shelf like so many other studies that preceded this one.

New Yorkers know what is wrong with their transit system and they also have the common sense to recommend improvements. The problem is that officials don't talk, much less listen, to the average Joe who rides the trains. However, if the panjandrums would listen, there is much that could be achieved to eliminate waste and improve safety.

It is obvious that neighborhoods in decline lose residents and subway riders. Yet the static nature of the system means that stops will be made even when there are relatively few riders. It is equally obvious that there are many places for muggers and other thugs to hide on stations and between subway cars. The rise in subway crime in the last decade gives substantial testimony to the claim that the New York underground is a breeding place for criminal activity.

While many proposals have been made to deal with the deplorable conditions, most are either very expensive, for example, additional cops, or foolhardy, for example, curtailing evening service. But what hasn't been tried and might very well work is consolidated late-hour service using express trains and express stops exclusively, with each train heavily manned with cops. If schedules of this late-hour express service were printed and coordinated—to the degree possible—with bus schedules, subway cops could be redeployed to express lines and only the express stations where trains would stop.

Under this plan there would be a modest reduction in service, particularly on local lines, but with this reduction there would be an opportunity to use all available subway patrolmen on express trains without any additional expense for the Transit Authority. Moreover, if the trains ran on a designated schedule, it might be possible to coordinate bus and subway service in the late evening hours.

The key to this proposal is reclaiming the subway system from thugs during the "low-use" period. This is often the time when violent crime occurs (albeit other kinds of crime have declined during the late evening hours), and it is clearly hazardous for any self-respecting citizen who is obliged to use the trains at an off-hour. Most important, this proposal sends a signal without any financial burden: the subway system will not be conceded to thugs after 11:00 P.M.

If such a plan were successful, it might encourage late-evening ridership. At the very least, consolidation will translate into more riders on those trains being used, which in itself would be an improvement on present conditions.

New York is very dependent on its transportation assets. City officials can't tell residents of this town to use public transportation in an effort to alleviate automobile traffic unless the subway system is efficient and safe. During the rush hours those conditions are often met. But in the off-hours the subway is converted into a social cesspool of violent crime and perversion. It is also a period when full service is offered in sparsely populated train cars, which in itself is a clear case of gross inefficiency.

There was a time three decades ago when I would travel on the subway at 2:00 or 3:00 A.M. from Queens to the farthest reaches in the Bronx. I could read my books without the slightest concern about what my fellow riders might be doing. Undoubtedly the times have changed; I wouldn't think of taking this trip in the late hours now. But it would be refreshing for New Yorkers to think that from 11:00 P.M. to 7:00 A.M. there is a plan to reclaim the subway from thugs. It would be eye-opening for the head of the Transit Authority to say, "We can guarantee your safety on these trains in the late evening and early morning hours. The subways belong to the people again, thugs beware."

June 22, 1988

90

The Fare-Beater Detail
on New York Subways

It is increasingly obvious that a significant proportion of New York's subway riders do not pay a fare. It is also evident that many of the thugs and other undesirables on the subway fall into the category of nonpaying riders. While the subway cops have done their best to curtail this practice, it goes on largely unabated. There simply aren't enough cops for the many illegal riders.

However, I have a self-paying, possibly profit-oriented, proposal to deal with this issue: a fare-beater detail organized as a separate subway force. As I see it, this detail would have the authority to detain fare-beaters and dispense fines up to $100. If violators don't pay their fines, their salaries should be garnisheed. Should cheaters continue the practice, the fine will double for a second offense; three-time losers will be barred from subway use up to three months, as is the case with offenders on the Paris Metro.

There is little doubt that this detail can easily pay for itself and possibly generate revenue. On most Manhattan stations the level of fare-beating is staggering. A low-level fence on the recently renovated IRT Astor Place station is a virtual invitation to cheat. Last week I observed a couple somewhat annoyed at the line for tokens. The male pointed to the fence and the two hopped over brazenly.

Many of the undesirables on the subway system are perennial fare-beaters. For these people, jumping the turnstile is a minor violation compared to their actions once on the trains. A residual effect of fining fare-beaters, or at least alerting them to that possibility, is the role this detail can have in making the subways somewhat safer for everyone. In fact even if this detail had a price tag for the city administration, it might be worthwhile. But there is every reason to believe it can easily pay for itself.

If present practices were to continue, daily gross revenue on the IRT alone between Astor Place and 86th Street should be on the order of $5,000 a day even if only 10 percent of the fare-beaters were apprehended. This detail would also have a salutary effect on the morale of other subway riders. I know how embittered I've become as I observe people break the law with as much aplomb as turning on their television sets.

In the last analysis this fare-beater detail can go a long way toward restoring civility to New York's public institutions. It is unfortunate that a breakdown of internalized civic responsibility necessitates external controls. But that is the only answer to what ails us; one can no longer simply plead for orderly behavior and moral rectitude. All the pleading in the world won't change the behavior of the growing army of New York's undesirables. The city administration must exercise its authority to keep the city safe and orderly for the rest of us.

While fare-beating certainly isn't a major crime, it is one of those activities that nibbles away at the fabric of social cohesion. Even basically decent people begin to ask, "Why am I the sap who pays when everyone else is getting a free ride?" From such questions anarchic responses spring. There are already too many areas of New York City life where civic order is in jeopardy of being discarded.

In some respects the fare-beater detail has symbolic value. This group of subway "meter maids" suggests that the city administration will not concede control of the subways to thugs. It also indicates that the so-called slippery slope of disorder can be reversed; there is nothing inevitable about anarchy. That point must be asserted and reasserted by the authorities; assuming control of the subways certainly conveys that message.

For some it may seem trifling to put so much emphasis on a fare-beater detail when there are serious crimes on the streets of this city. Needless to say I am not oblivious to the heinous crime on the street, much of it unsolved and unpunished. But it seems to me important to note that minor crime has its corrosive influence on city life as well. The acceptance of fare-beating is merely one poignant sign of civic decay. It is a very short ride between the acceptance of minor crime and turning one's back on major crime.

There isn't likely to be an outcry of support for a fare-beater detail, primarily because New Yorkers have adapted to the illegal practice on our subways the way they've adapted to drug dealing in our parks. But if put to a vote and framed as a no-cost or low-cost budgetary item, this would be a most welcome addition to municipal affairs. I know it would do a great deal for my spirit to see the regular fence-hoppers at the Astor Place station fined by a plainclothes member of the fare-beater patrol. If New York can have its evil spirits extinguished by ghostbusters in the person of Bill Murray and company, I don't see why it can't have its fare-beaters removed by fare-busters hired to sustain the law, keep our subways free of thugs, and restore morale to those New Yorkers who still abide by the law.

August 31, 1988

91

Parking Meters in Manhattan: Reexamining a Mistaken Impression

While reforms in New York appear at breakneck speed, their introduction rarely leads to evaluation. How can those who propose a reform put their political lives on the line by admitting they were wrong? The consequence is that the reform of yesterday is a permanent fixture of tomorrow.

In the 1970s most of the parking meters were removed from the streets of Manhattan. This was done for good reason: meters, it was argued at the time, encouraged drivers into Manhattan, and parked cars removed one lane from many thoroughfares. While the city administration would lose revenue because of this move, it could reduce traffic, pump commercial vitality into Manhattan, and reduce rush-hour gridlock.

That none of these things has occurred can't be attributed to the reformers. They meant well and their logic was impeccable. The problem, however, is that even though this reform has failed, no one can admit to being wrong.

New Yorkers use their cars because they don't have confidence in public transportation. It is better to sit in traffic on the Brooklyn-Queens Expressway, than put your life on the line on the "D" Train. While that is unquestionably an exaggerated view, it is widely accepted. One would assume that the astronomical price for parking would discourage drivers to Manhattan, but that is the opposite of what is happening. Drivers are generally insensitive to financial disincentives because they can't place a dollar tag on their life and safety.

Since the reform is not working and since Manhattan needs parking spaces and revenues for municipal services, I would propose that parking meters be reinstalled. I would also propose that every cent raised in this manner be spent on public transportation, most particularly the subway system.

Most critics of this proposal will contend that parked cars will exacerbate Manhattan's traffic woes. Yet traffic is caused not only by many cars, but many cars double- and triple-parked. If anything, meters could alleviate this condition, since meter maids will ticket those cars whose time limit has expired.

Rarely is a double-parked car ticketed. In fact the reasons traffic has worsened since the 1970s is not only the increased number of cars on the road, but the ubiquitous double-parking violations in Manhattan. To cite one example, the double-parked cars from Houston Streets to Canal Street on Broadway have converted "the great white way" into a veritable obstacle course with only one lane available for moving vehicles.

Admittedly it is hard to say you were wrong. No one likes to do it. The year 1989, after all, is a mayoral election year. But consider if you will the ramifications of this decision. New York would have additional resources for public transportation. If less than prevailing market rates are charged, $2 an hour can be collected, a windfall for the public coffers. Traffic conditions couldn't possibly worsen and might even improve. And New Yorkers would appreciate the recognition of a reform that went wrong and can be reexamined by an open-minded city administration.

As is the case is most city matters, the impediment to change is will. When city officials start scurrying about to find new sources of revenue this idea may gain support. Until then I suspect my proposal will languish along with many other notions that would force politicans to admit they made a mistake.

October 19, 1988

92

"Sunshine Laws" in New York

I recently found myself on the East River Drive in the middle of a rainstorm. Caught in the usual traffic snarl, I noticed that a flood was surrounding my car and those nearby. There was little I could do about the matter short of abandoning my automobile. Then it struck me; this is the same East Side Drive that has been undergoing repair, expansion, and improvement for the last year; the East Side Drive that represents the only highway in Manhattan and a roadway that has cost the citizens of this town millions of dollars in tax-levied funds. How can it be that with all the work done and all the money spent, this highway is so badly flawed?

The reason for this condition is that in New York there isn't any account-ability for work done on our streets and highways. Contracts aren't given out for outstanding performance; they are rewarded as a form of patronage, a quid pro quo for campaign contributions and knowing the right people.

However, there is a way out of this morass. The agency responsible for highway maintenance in New York should cite contractors for improper work. Those cited should appear on a public list available to anyone who inquires about it. The "sunshine" provision should be incorporated into every contract the city consummates with a private firm.

In the process of exposing those culpable for flawed work, the mayor can also determine which contractors are rehired despite their less than adequate performance. That the city is ripped off is hardly surprising. Some things never change. The story of the construction of a new City Hall during the era of Boss Tweed makes present-performance contracts seem like penny-ante stuff.

But it is interesting, and revealing, that some roads in New York are under permanent construction. The Belt Parkway has always been under repair. It is quite literally a road that has, for as long as I can remember, been under construction. Notice I am not referring to the potholes that require fixing. Salting the roads in winter and the constant barrage of heavy trucks take their expected toll. I am referring instead to those roads with serious structural flaws that result in flooding or those roads that are never completed, like the much discussed East Side subway tunnel to nowhere.

New York is perhaps one of the few places where it is possible to do shoddy work and still be rehired. There is obviously more at stake here than a road. The only way to change matters is through a public awareness of the problem. At the moment few people are aware of the identity of contractors, even though almost every motorist is aware of the construction flaws.

The public listing I am proposing is not dissimilar to the listing of misdeeds in the Puritan community. Since government controls don't work or are insufficiently applied, social censure might be a useful corrective. It also makes sense to compare those on a list for shoddy work with those who have made campaign contributions.

In the end accountability is the only way to improve New York's services. With a city as large and complex as this one, much will inevitably fall between the stools either intentionally or unintentionally. Therefore open disclosure is the only real protection the average person has against bureaucratic malfeasance or inertia. It is foolhardy to assume that the city administration of its own volition will prosecute and censure those who haven't fulfilled the responsibilities of their contract.

New York needs its own version of "sunshine laws" so that contractors can be held accountable and city administrations can be kept honest. If this seems excessive, ask yourself the next time you're caught in both a traffic jam and a rainstorm on the East River Drive: Why doesn't the drainage system work after the expenditure of millions of taxpayers' dollars on "road improvements"?

December 14, 1988

93

A Citizens' Campaign to Reconstitute New York

Recapturing New York from the barbarians in our midst won't be an easy chore. But if a campaign is to begin in which one institution a month is reclaimed, here are my suggestions for the city administration. I heartily concur with my colleagues at the *New York Post* that Washington Square Park should be the first institution restored to decent people. But that would be little more than a beginning in pushing back the tide of criminality.

I would recommend that movie-theater owners rehire matrons, women who are presently receiving city welfare payments, so that decorous behavior in our theaters is restored and decent people don't have to contend with dope- and crack-smoking viewers who don't have the slightest qualms about disturbing their neighbors.

I would recommend that the restrooms on the subway at 42nd Street and Lexington Avenue be returned to decent, law-abiding citizens. The restrooms must be cleaned, fumigated, and patrolled.

I would recommend the reissue of billy clubs to cops on a beat. That club was a very powerful deterrent as it was twirled artfully by the cop near my favorite teenage hangout.

I would recommend that the Bowery be restored as the vagrant center in New York. If vagrants are in one place instead of wandering aimlessly throughout the city, aid can be offered. I would also suggest that in place of the "deinstitutionalization" movement, we have a "reinstitutionalization" movement for those who are mentally incompetent and unable to care for themselves.

I would recommend that a place near the ocean be reacquired where kids can go on rides and adults can walk on the boardwalk without being hassled or robbed. It might even be called Steeplechase II. To make sure the parachute ride will operate again, I would give the concession to negligence lawyers.

I would recommend that one waiting area for travelers be provided at the Port Authority where decent people can avoid the gauntlet of pimps, vagrants, and drug dealers.

I would recommend that one subway line be made secure, say the IRT, twenty-four hours a day. One might even offer a free ride after midnight to encourage riders in the late hours. But that assumes every car of every train on this line will be patrolled by a subway cop from midnight to 7:00 A.M.

I would recommend that one public swimming pool be secured. New York deserves to have one pool that isn't controlled by creeps and thugs. I would recommend the Aquacade in Flushing Meadow Park, a place where Billy Rose once dazzled New Yorkers with his spectacular shows.

I would recommend that one evening program at a city university be made secure so that people who work during the day can once again take advantage of evening courses. My obvious candidate is City College of New York (CCNY), a place that educated several generations of New Yorkers with its evening classes. In this case, cops would have to be strategically placed from the Broadway subway station to the CCNY campus.

I would recommend a return to street cleaners who pick up litter from our streets instead of mechanized sweepers that push garbage from one side of the street to the other. In making this suggestion, it is hoped that clean streets might dissuade barbarians from throwing their litter on the already present garbage pile. Although there are some street cleaners with shovel and pail, there aren't enough to demonstrate what it takes in human effort to keep New York clean from the assault of litterbugs.

I would recommend that the city use the 100,000 abandoned buildings it owns as prison cells for the drug dealers who are waiting to be sentenced. Rather than have tax dollars pay for the rehabilitation of these buildings, I would use the army of 28,000 drug dealers waiting for trial as the construction workers for their own cells. This might give these young men something constructive to do and it most certainly would assist the judges who seem to be reluctant to sentence dealers because of overcrowded conditions on Rikers Island.

That does it; twelve suggestions, one a month, to restore a semblance of civility to a city in desperate need of a boost. This plan is certainly no panacea, but then again, there are no panaceas on the horizon. What New Yorkers need is a belief that entropy can be contained, that there is a possibility islands of order can be recreated. This plan, it seems to me, might go a long way toward restoring New York's hopefulness.

March 5, 1987